RURAL COOPERATION

In The Cooperative Movement in Tanzania

RURAL COOPERATION

In The Cooperative Movement in Tanzania

Francis Fanuel Lyimo

PUBLISHED BY
Mkuki na Nyota Publishers Ltd
Nyerere Road, Quality Plaza Building
P. O. Box 4246
Dar es Salaam, Tanzania
www.mkukinanyota.com
publish@mkukinanyota.com

Cover Photo: Sofia Henriques

ISBN 978 9987 08 155 4

Contents

Acronyms and Abbreviations

(ACU)	Arusha Cooperative Union
(BNCU)	Bukoba Native Cooperative Union
(CAT)	Coffee Authority of Tanzania
(CATA)	Cashewnut Authority of Tanzania
(CCM)	Chama Cha Mapinduzi
(CDD)	Cooperative Development Division
(COASCO)	Cooperative Audit and Supervision Corporation
(CRDB)	Cooperative Rural Development Bank
(CUT)	Cooperative Union of Tanganyika
(DCD)	Department of Cooperative Development
(GAPEX)	National Agricultural Product Export Corporation
(GDP)	Gross Domestic Product
(GNP)	Gross National Product
(ICA)	International Cooperative Alliance
(ILO)	International Labour Organization
(KNCU)	Kilimanjaro Native Cooperative Union
(KNPA)	Kilimanjaro Native Planters Association

(LSMB)	Lint and Seed Marketing Board
(MA)	Master of Arts
(MCU)	Meru Cooperative Union
(MORECU)	Morogoro Regional Cooperation Union
(NAPB)	National Agricultural Products Board
(NCDB)	National Cooperative and Development Bank
(NCU)	Nyanza Cooperative Union
(NGOMAT)	Ngoni – Matengo Cooperative Union
(NMC)	National Milling Corporation
(PhD)	Doctor of Philosophy
(RACU)	Rungwe African Cooperative Union
(RTC)	Regional Trading Company
(SACCOS)	Savings and Credit Cooperative Societies
(SHIREC)	Shinyanga Regional Cooperative Union
(TACTA)	Tanganyika Cooperative Trading Agency
(TANU)	Tanganyika African National Union
(TARECU)	Tanga Regional Cooperative Union
(TAT)	Tobacco Authority of Tanzania
(TCA)	Tanzania Cotton Authority
(TCB)	Tanganyika Coffee Board
(TCGA)	Tanganyika Coffee Growers Association
(TRDB)	Tanzania Rural Development Bank
(TTA)	Tanzania Tea Authority
(UCS)	Union of Cooperative Societies
(URT)	United Republic of Tanzania
(USA)	United States of America
(VFCU)	Victoria Federation of Cooperative Unions

Acknowledgements

Financial sponsorship from the Kilimanjaro Native Cooperative Union Ltd covered tuition and fees for my studies at the University of Dar es Salaam for my Master of Arts degree in Sociology. A United States government scholarship paid for my studies at the University of Wisconsin–Madison to pursue my Doctor of Philosophy degree in Sociology and Rural Sociology with a minor in Agricultural Economics, in which I specialized in the study of cooperatives. These opportunities laid the foundation for my endeavor to do more research and write about cooperation and the cooperative movement.

During the preparation of the manuscript I incurred both intellectual and personal debts. I am grateful to all authors whose work has been referenced in this book. The scale of my indebtedness to earlier writers is judged by the frequency with which I refer to their works.

Over the past seven years I have exchanged views on Rural Cooperation and Rural Development at seminars in the Department of Sociology and Anthropology at the University of Dar es Salaam. Seminars were a source of stimulation in my work. I am indebted at least as much to my colleagues at the University for the ideas they contributed, and which I acknowledge with gratitude.

I appreciate the support and encouragement of Julitha Lyimo and Tumainiel Lyimo, who always helped me to get over the hurdles of researching and writing this book. I couldn't have done it without them.

Finally I thank Ms Dorothy Mariki, who typed the work several times.

Preface

I have lectured a course on Rural Cooperation in Tanzania at the University of Dar es Salaam for seven consecutive years. However, lack of appropriate books with adequate coverage of the course content obliged me to conduct extensive research on cooperation and cooperatives. This material evolved and became the basis for this book about Rural Cooperation in Tanzania. The book covers the entire field and addresses the subject by providing a foundation on which wider study can be based. It is intended to make its readers aware of the strategies and challenges of cooperation and has a wider relevance, as it will be useful to policy makers in the cooperative sector, which is a significant part of the private sector in Tanzania, and indeed in most African countries.

The research foundation for this book is reflected in the bibliography found at the end of every chapter. In the same spirit, research was done on documentary data on cooperation and cooperative development. Analysis and interpretation of the researched information reflect my original contributions in the book. The analysis attempted does not conceal the weaknesses and deficiencies in the cooperative movement in Tanzania.

The topics included make it appropriate for use in Sociology, Rural Development, Marketing, Development Studies and studies in other specialties in the Social Sciences.

1

Definitions and Meaning of Cooperative Organization

Aristotle recognized the social nature of human beings. He believed that a person could not lead a happy and contented life if that person lived in isolation. A person needs the company, help and support of others. Therefore, there is a great need for cooperation among human beings, which can be considered as the basic principle underlying human life. (Sharada, V. 1984: 3) No person, no country in the world, irrespective of its stage of development, is fully self-sufficient. It is cooperation that motivates and directs human life towards the pursuit of peace and prosperity. Cooperation brings together peoples and nations and facilitates peaceful co-existence.

1.1 Definitions of Cooperative Organisation

R. Phillips defines a cooperative as a business association of firms or households, and an economic institution through which economic activity is conducted in the pursuit of economic objectives (Sharada, V. 1984: 7) This definition does not say anything about the functioning of a cooperative society. It does not show how a cooperative society is distinguished from other business organizations.

J.P. Warbasse defines cooperation as a way of life whereby people unite democratically in the spirit of mutual aid to get the largest possible access to things and services that they need. (Sharada, V. 1984: 8). This definition is narrow in scope, for it contains only two characteristics of a cooperative society, namely, mutual help and democratic management.

Paul Casselman defined a cooperative as an economic system with a social content. (Schaars, M.A. 1971: 7) It means that people come together voluntarily to perform some activities for their own benefits. A true cooperative is defined as a business, voluntarily organized, operating at cost and which is owned and controlled by member patrons, sharing risks and benefits proportional to their participation (Roy E, 1969).

The International Cooperative Alliance (ICA), which has been the final authority since its creation in 1895[1] for defining cooperatives and for elaborating cooperative principles, offered the following definition in 1995 : "A cooperative is an autonomous association of persons united voluntarily to meet their common economic, social and cultural needs and aspirations through a jointly owned and democratically controlled enterprise" (Prakash 2003: 4).

1.2 Meaning of Cooperative Organization

Cooperatives are voluntary business organizations owned and controlled by their members who also receive benefits and services provided by those

1 The reformulation of the former two formal declarations of 1937 and 1966 was an attempt to interpret cooperative principles in the contemporary world.

businesses. Cooperatives are enterprises that put people, and not capital, at the center of their business. Cooperatives are business enterprises, which can be defined in terms of the three basic interests of ownership, control and benefit. Only in the cooperative enterprise are all three interests vested directly in the hands of the users. Cooperatives follow a broader set of values than those associated with purely making a profit. Because cooperatives are owned and democratically controlled by their members, the decisions taken by cooperatives balance the needs for profitability with the needs of their members and the wider interests of the community.

A cooperative is a business that is voluntarily owned and controlled by its member patrons, and which is operated for them and by them on a non-profit or cost basis (Schaars M.A. 1971: 7). A cooperative is organized and incorporated to engage in economic activities according to ideals of democracy, social consciousness and human relations.

A cooperative provides services and benefits to its members in proportion to the use they make of their organization. It is not a welfare agency or a charitable and benevolent society. It depends upon income earned from rendering services to meet its expenses rather than upon donations, government funds or support from philanthropic organizations. Services paid for by its member patrons are its primary orientation. The primary goal of a cooperative is to meet members' needs in an economical, efficient manner.

1.3 Features which Distinguish a Cooperative from other Business Enterprises

a) The cooperative organization provides economic benefits to member patrons which include educational, social or other benefits;

b) The cooperative business is essentially a non-profit enterprise. A cooperative benefits users of its services rather than making a profit for the organization or for the members as investors;

c) The cooperative is controlled by the people who use it. Generally, every member is given a single vote irrespective of the volume of business they contract with the organization; and

d) The cooperative is centered on the mutual interests of its members, that is, around a bond of common interest. (Schaars, M.A. 1971: 7)

1.4 Cooperative Policies

a) Risks, costs, and benefits are shared equitably among members;

b) Members have an obligation to patronize their cooperative; and

c) Business is done primarily, not necessarily exclusively, with members (Schaars, M.A. 1971: 7).

1.5 Basic Concepts in Cooperative Societies

Basic to any cooperative organization is the spirit of voluntarism and the element of proportionality. These two concepts are foundation blocks upon which the cooperative structure rests.

The idea of cooperating presupposes the voluntary action of those involved. Coercion is the antithesis of cooperation. True cooperation with others is a feeling that comes from the heart. In true cooperatives, persons are free to join if they wish and leave when they want to do so. This is the spirit of voluntarism. When people cooperate they share with one another the risks, responsibilities, duties, rights and benefits of their collective effort. No one person or segment bears the total responsibility or obtains all the benefits. All are involved in giving and taking, furnishing and sharing, risking and benefiting. On what basis are business losses and benefits apportioned? The basis is according to the proportion or percent of business done through the cooperative organization.

Cooperatives are based on cooperative values such as self-help, self-responsibility, democracy, equality, equity and solidarity. Furthermore, early cooperative founders followed special "ethical values" such as honesty, openness, social responsibility and caring for others. Members of cooperatives believe that in association with others, full individual development can take place. While all people should strive to control their own destiny, self-responsibility includes also the responsibility for their cooperative, including its establishment, its continuing vitality and independence. Members finance their cooperative, meet its operating costs, and share the savings and losses on this basis (Schaars, M.A 1971: 7-8).

1.6 Basic Principles of Cooperatives

The following principles identify business-type cooperatives. There are three basic principles and four supplementary principles. (Schaars, M.A. 1971: 8-10)

a) Control by member users

This basic principle is also called democratic member control.

Each member is generally limited to one vote on each issue voted upon, regardless of how much stock the member owns or how much business the member conducts with the cooperative. Voting on a one-member one-vote basis is not in accordance with the concept of proportionality;

b) Operations on a cost-of-doing business basis

The second basic principle is achieved by charging patrons only the actual cost of performing a service. If there are overcharges, these are returned to patrons in proportion to the business they conducted with the cooperative. The cooperative is not operated to profit at the expense of its member patrons. Any excess income over expenses, called "profit" in a regular corporation and "net savings", "net income" or "net earnings" in a cooperative is returned as Patronage Refunds to the member patrons pursuant to a mandatory contract to do so. Such a mandatory contract is usually included in the by-laws or by resolution. It establishes that any excess income over expenses belongs to the patrons and is not the property of the organization. The return of the overcharges actually reduces the gross income and places the cooperative on a cost-of-doing business basis; and

c) Limited dividends

The third basic principle is limited dividends, which are intended to keep the cooperative operating. The return on the investment is called a "dividend" and not "interest". Interest payments are operating expenses, dividends are not. Dividends are paid from net earnings and, if there are none, no payments can be made without impairing the capital of the cooperative.

In 1966 the International Cooperative Alliance (ICA) decided that the following four supplementary principles, in addition to the three basic principles mentioned above, should be considered essential to genuine and effective cooperative practice.

a) Membership should be voluntary and available without artificial restriction or any social, racial, political or religious discrimination to all persons who can make use of cooperative services and are willing to accept the responsibilities of membership (open membership and the principle of political, racial and religious neutrality);
b) Surplus or savings, if any, belong to the members and should be distributed in proportion to the business of each member with the cooperative (the patronage refund principle);
c) All cooperatives should educate their members, officers, employees and the general public in the principles and techniques of cooperation (the principle of promotion of education); and
d) All cooperative organizations, to best serve their members and their communities, should actively cooperate in every practical way with other cooperatives at local, national and international levels. (Schaars, M.A. 1971: 9-10).

1.7 Similarities of Cooperative with Non-Cooperative Business

In some respects cooperatives are like the non-cooperative businesses with which they must compete. Among similarities are the following:

a) Cooperative and non-cooperative business enters the labour, capital and management markets and must pay the same wages, same interest rates and comparable compensation for management;

b) Many operational practices are the same, such as packaging, storing, transportation, processing, granting of credit, advertising and pricing;

c) Both types of business aim to improve their efficiency and operate economically; and

d) Both cooperative and non-cooperative businesses may be located in an area with the same general economic factors– employment and unemployment, tightening or loosening of credit, inflation and deflation, taxes and changes in consumption patterns affecting both.

1.8 Differences Between Cooperative and Non–cooperative Business

The differences are primarily in the relationship between the owners and their organization and in the way profits and net savings are distributed. In this contrast we focus on corporations and cooperatives.

a) Purpose

Corporations

- To earn profit for investors and increase the value of shares
- To serve the public generally

Cooperatives

- To maximize net and real income of member users and provide goods and/or services at cost to member users
- To serve the members primarily

b) Organization

Corporations

- Incorporated under state corporate law
- Organized and owned by investors
- Stock of a large corporation is sold on the stock exchange

Cooperatives

- Organized under state cooperative law
- Organized around mutual interest of its member users
- Organized and owned by member users

c) Control

Corporations

- By investors, the stockholders
- Policies determined by stockholders and directors voting on the basis of stock ownership according to the number of shares held
- Proxy voting permitted

Cooperative
- By member patrons
- Policies made by member users and directors
- Voting in local associations usually on a one-member one-vote basis
- No proxy voting

d) Sources of Capital

Corporations
- From investing public
- From successful business operations with profits reinvested

Cooperatives
- From member users
- From net earnings on successful operations with reinvestment of part or all of the profits

e) Distribution of Net Margins

Corporations
- To stockholders in proportion to number of shares of stock held

Cooperatives
- To patrons on a patronage basis after modest dividends on stock have been paid

f) Stock dividends

Corporations
- No limit and depends on amount of profit and distribution policy

Cooperatives
- Limited to a nominal amount

g) Operating Practices

Corporations
- Use conventional methods of financing: sale of stock, issuance of bonds, bank loans, and reinvestment of part of the profits
- Usually purchase products on a cash basis
- Business done with public generally
- Primarily interested in operational efficiency to cut costs and are less interested in pricing efficiency
- Charge competitive prices

Cooperatives

- Use revolving capital plan of financing based on the amount of business transacted with patrons in addition to conventional financing procedures
- Usually pool receipts and pay average prices by grade for products received
- Business done primarily using marketing contracts made exclusively with members
- Not only interested in operational efficiency but in pricing efficiency as well so that differential pricing by grade may reveal to producers ultimate consumer preferences, tastes, and purchases
- Charge either competitive or break-even prices in purchasing associations (Schaas M.A. (1971: 11)

References

Abrahamsen, M.A., 1976, *Cooperative Business Enterprise,* New York: McGraw-Hill Book Company.

Andrew, P., 1977, *Cooperative Institutions and Economic Development, Union of Manitoba, Canada,* Nairobi: East Africa Literature Bureau.

Digby, M., 1990, *The World Cooperative Movement,* London: Hutchinson and Co Ltd.

Hyden, G., 1973, *Efficiency versus Distribution in East African Cooperatives. A Study in Organizational Conflicts,* Uppsala: East African Studies.

Laidlaw, A.F., 1974, *The Cooperative Sector,* Columbia: University of Missouri Press.

Prakash, D., 2003, *The Principles of Cooperation A Look at the ICA Cooperative Identity Statement,* New Delhi: Rural Development and Management Centre.

Roy. E.P., 1969, *Cooperatives Today and Tomorrow,* Danville, Illinois: The Interstates Printers and Publishers, Inc.

Schaars, M.A., 1971, *Cooperative Principles and Practices,* Madison: University of Wisconsin Cooperative Extension.

Sharada, V., 1984, *The Theory of Cooperation,* Bombay: Himalaya Publishing House.

Strickland, C.F., 1933, *Cooperation for Africa,* London: Oxford University Press.

Young, C. Neal S. and Tim H. R. 1981, *Cooperatives and Development. Agricultural Politics in Ghana and Uganda,* London: Oxford University Press.

2

Cooperative Thought and Evolution of Cooperatives

Historians have found evidence of cooperation in ancient Greece, Egypt, Rome, Babylon, and China. Early agriculture would have been impossible without some elementary forms of cooperation, as people relied on one another to defend land, harvest crops, build storage buildings and to share equipment. However, it wasn't until the pressures of poverty caused by the Industrial Revolution resulted in critical thinking and experiments toward the development of the cooperative as we know it today. In this chapter we discuss cooperative thought by focusing on the major scholars and their contributions to the idea.

2.1 Pre-Rochdale Period

Prior to the Industrial Revolution (1750-1850) most families were largely self-sufficient. The Industrial Revolution introduced the factory system of production, using machines instead of labour which gradually replaced a domestic system of cottage industries and home craftsmanship. The revolution brought expanded production, lowered prices, increased consumption and raised living standards. Its incipient commercial economy ushered in wages, prices, money, credit, transportation and sales, and employers and employees as distinct classes emerged. However, the modern factory system led to the exploitation of workers, the creation of many socio-economic problems and it hampered the tradition of self-sufficient agricultural production as workers congregated around large cities. Because they were engaged in the long hours of factory work, the employees became dependent upon others for provisions, housing and other necessities.

Not only was there a revolution in industry but a revolution had already been underway in agriculture during the 17th and 18th centuries. Scattered field strips and land previously cropped were made into large estates to pasture sheep and other livestock – extensive instead of intensive agriculture. Between 1750 and 1843 nearly 7 million acres of land were enclosed in England so that large numbers of small farmers were driven off the land. There was a revolution in ideas and a demand for personal rights.

In the years of the Industrial Revolution and after, merchants, artisans, and craftsmen took action in different ways to alleviate the distress they experienced. People tried to help themselves through guilds. Workers also organized into labour unions to bargain with employers and to promote favourable labour legislation.

2.2 Action to Alleviate Distress

The government of England passed inadequate and badly administered laws as public relief measures to alleviate the depressed condition of the masses. Philanthropists also aided by purchasing flour and meal and distributing it at wholesale prices to the poor. By operating corn mills at cost or without charge, and supplying fuel, clothing and basic staples at cost, they contributed to the poor but such help was totally inadequate.

In addition to these measures, workers helped themselves:

a) Guilds, which were associations of merchants, artisans, craftsmen and others with mutual interests, set up rules and regulations binding their members to their production or business operations and supported them financially during sickness, family hardship or other crises.

b) Workers organized labour unions to bargain with employers and to promote favourable labour legislation.

c) Workers organized cooperative associations for the production of commodities, the purchase of consumer goods, and to provide cooperative housing (Schaars, M.A. 1971: 66).

2.3 Early Cooperative Societies

Cooperation existed in business prior to the Industrial Revolution and the most successful attempts were in insurance. There are records of mutual fire insurance companies in London and Paris as early as 1530, but the first highly successful society was the Amicable Society organized in England in 1705. Cooperative industrial enterprises occurred in England as early as 1760. Most of these early cooperatives were consumer-controlled organizations for flour milling and baking.

These organizations failed to attract much attention until the early 19th century when a prominent industrialist named Robert Owen (1777–1858) began to advocate for the establishment of cooperative communities to alleviate the suffering of industrial workers. Owen had grandiose ideas encompassing agricultural and industrial production, education, housing and commercial distribution on cooperative bases.

2.4 Evolution of Cooperative Thought

After the early cooperatives failed, other pioneers contributed to the evolution of cooperatives. Robert Owen was among the earlier famous cooperative pioneers. Owen's idea was that Cooperative Societies ought to be self-sufficient communities based on the production of goods and services for consumption. Digby wrote:

> *Owen, with his own success before his eyes and perhaps belles tracts on his desk, should look to the development of sound economic and social life through self-constrained and verbally self-sufficient communities or colonies (Digby, M. 1990: 13).*

Owen was credited with developing a "new view of society", which he described in his widely recognized essays. The first essay developed his belief that "Man's character is made for him and not by him". His second and third essays described in detail the economic system at his textile mills in New Lanark, Scotland and the educational programme he developed there. It was his view that education was basic to the success of any programme and could be relied upon to facilitate giant steps in eliminating poverty, misery and crime.

Owen retired from business to devote all his time to his social theories. The real association lies, however, more in his ultimate ideals than in his immediate plan for organization. His central plan was for self-supporting communities such as Fourrier's Phalanstère, where producers and consumers were one and the same rather than dividing society into classes of consumers and producers. He tried to bring people together by organizing Grand National Consolidated Trade Unions, which had more than 500,000 members. The movements tried to reorganize industry along cooperative lines. The union collapsed but he continued to write and agitate for government aid, although his plans were not accepted. His ideas influenced later cooperative movements.

Owen knew by practical experience the Industrial Revolution's effect on the working class. He argued for production by voluntary association on a non-profit basis, and approved of the few short-lived cooperatives that existed prior to the foundation of the Rochdale Society. He was also the first to apply the term "cooperative" to these activities, and may be accepted as the father of the cooperative movement. He denounced competition because it lead to exploitation, and advocated in its place a system based on village cooperation in which men and women worked together for the mutual benefit of their labour.

Owen was very influential in the development of initial concepts for cooperative communities in order to overcome economic depression and unemployment. He believed the process of industrialization was going to grow steadily. Because of that he saw a need for new models that could correct the ailments of the industrial society, models that could become cooperatives. According to Owen the ideal group or community should consist of 500 to 3000 people placed on about 1500 acres. All community members would occupy one large building containing a public kitchen and mess room, and with a separate apartment for each family.

Owen's experience at New Lanark encouraged him to deal with the impact of the Industrial Revolution by advocating for communal cooperative villages that would largely be self-sufficient in character. In this framework, he created an environment in which the following four basic cooperative ideas emerged in embryonic form:

a) Associated effort–Owen's thinking centered on bringing people together in an effort to deal with the problems confronting them;
b) Voluntary approach–people were free to join or not. Owen believed that through educational efforts many of them would come to understand the merits of his ideas;
c) Democratic control–after understanding the objectives of his cooperative ventures Owen believed that people could be relied upon to make the right decisions in terms of governing themselves; and
d) Service to members emphasized that a communal society should identify member needs and should seek to satisfy them. Production would be for use and not for profit.

When evaluated in terms of their contribution to cooperative enterprise today, the ideas advocated by Owen differ in three basic respects (Abrahamsen, M.A. 1976: 72):

a) Society in Owen's self-sufficient communities would be based only on the production of goods and services for personal use. Today's cooperatives however, are highly specialized: they restrict operations to specific member needs and are very much a part of the exchange economy;
b) Owen thought in terms of joint ownership of property, a community with common interests and joint sharing of benefits. Modern cooperative operations, in contrast, are oriented towards the accumulation of private property and the sharing of benefits in proportion to one's participation in the business; and
c) Owen depended on philanthropists for capital. Today members are expected to provide a substantial share of the necessary capital to start and operate their cooperative (Abrahamsen M.A 1976: 73).

Some of Owen's contemporaries also contributed to cooperative thought, often by reinforcing or slightly modifying his ideas.

Dr. William King (1786 – 1865) was a physician in Brighton, England. In 1827, Dr. King organized a consumer cooperative at Brighton that was to serve as a model for hundreds of local societies in the 1830s. He emphasized that:

a) Cooperatives are voluntary and not compulsory (Abrahamsen, M.A. 1976: 73); and
b) Cooperatives should be neutral in terms of political and religious convictions. His publication "The Cooperator" was so influential that it became a textbook of sorts for the early Cooperative Movement.

Digby (1990) wrote that, like Owen, Dr. King preached the supreme value of labour but also saw the importance of capital, which he regarded as the product of labour put in a reserve. More democratic than Owen, Dr. King was all for self-help and no patronage from the rich (ibid.).

While Owen and King were propagating cooperative theory in England, similar ideas were finding their way into print in France. The French Revolution (1789) brought tremendous changes to the lives of the people and the ideas of that time. François Charles Fourier (1772-1837), a commercial traveler and visionary, had a great impact on cooperative thought. He was the inventor of the phalanxes: agricultural communities which had an economic function and a social role (Digby, M. 1990: 18).

Fourier was one of the original communal city planners, advocating groups of associated people living on land owned in common and in rationally-constructed communities. He placed special emphasis on agricultural production and on the reduction of distribution costs. Fourier called his concept of communal association a "Phalanx", which was a utopian community which needed three square miles for living. Each Phalanx would contain among other things social, educational and individual centers. Members had joint ownership over communal property, and the right to work for the common good rather than to earn profit. Even more than Owen, he stressed democracy in governing the phalanxes and voluntary association for participants. Below is an excerpt of his writing on the organization of his communities:

> *The Phalanx will produce an amount of wealth tenfold greater then the present. The system allows for a multitude of economies of operations and sales which will increase the return enormously. It requires a tract of land three miles square, well-watered, flanked by a forest. As women and children all work, there will be no idlers, all will earn more than they consume. Universal happiness and gaiety will reign. A unity of interests and views will arise, crime and violence disappear. The Phalanx will be devoted to the service of useful labour, of the sciences, the arts, and of the culinary department (Digby, M. 1990).*

Owen had, at about the same time Fourier developed his ideas in France, proposed the idea of a harmonic colony which was similar to Fourier's utopian community. The community should be mainly agricultural but should carry on other occupations to ensure self-sufficiency. The self-help and mutual-help concepts implied by the ideas of Fourier and Owen, despite their failure in a number of experiments, had formed a very important base which was used in the establishment of cooperatives in later years. However, all these early concepts failed due to a missing analysis of the social and historical setting. Furthermore, the early experiments often took place in idealistic communities set apart from society (Prakash 2003).

Simon's follower Phillippe Buckez (1796-1865), a doctor, also preached self-help and the accumulation of capital to be used for controlling and reforming the social economy. While King thought mainly about consumers purchasing to fulfill their needs, Buckez thought of producers selling the products of their labour. Thus Buckez applied ideas of associated enterprise, proportional returns, indivisible capital and limitation in the employment of labour for non-affiliated labour, which are ideas accepted by modern cooperative theorists. (Abrahamsen, 1976: 72-73).

The contributions made by these writers were inspired by the impact of the Industrial Revolution and, to overcome the problems it caused they emphasized two major concepts which were later taken up by cooperative business ventures. These ideas are: voluntary membership, and control by participants. Owen and his contemporaries influenced the Rochdale pioneers of 1844.

2.5 The Rochdale Pioneers

During this early period of cooperative development, one of the societies which sprung up in 1833, but failed in 1835 was at Rochdale, England. Dr King's writings might have influenced this early cooperative because James Smithies, one of the leaders among the 28 Rochdalians, was inspired by King's publication, "The Cooperator", and showed it to his fellow Rochdalians. This determined group continued to work actively for social reform even after the cooperative's failure.

Then in 1844 a consumer's cooperative store started in Rochdale, and it provided organizational and operating patterns that became the prototype for other consumers' cooperatives, both at the retail and wholesale levels, all over the world. The 28 Rochdalians had high hopes and aspirations. They hoped not only to establish a store for the sale of provisions but also to acquire homes in which their members might live. They had the following plans:

a) To manufacture articles that society needed;
b) To promote employment;
c) To acquire land on which to produce;
d) To produce products needed by members; and
e) To employ those members who were out of work or those whose wages were very low.

The Rochdalians wanted to "establish a self-supporting home colony of united interests" and to "arrange the powers of production, distribution, education and government" in the interest of its members and finally, "for the promotion of sobriety a temperance hotel [was] to be opened in one of the society's houses as soon as convenient". This was an ambitious program and it was very different from the purposes which cooperatives today state as their reason for organizing (Schaars, M.A. 1971: 68).

Taken separately, the business practices (later called Rochdalian principles) which these pioneers laid down for operating their little store on Toad Lane were not novel but the combination of all of them was essentially new.

These practices were:

a) Capital should be of their own providing and bear a fixed rate of interest (limited return on equity capital);
b) Only the purest provisions procurable should be supplied to members (to do away with abominable adulteration of food);
c) Full weight and measure should be given (to provide honesty in weighing);
d) Market prices should be charged and no credit given nor asked (cash trading, no charge accounts, charge prevailing prices);
e) Profit should be divided in proportion to the amount of purchases made by each member (patronage refunds);
f) The principles of "one-member, one-vote" should prevail in government, and the equality of the sexes in membership (democratic control);
g) Management should be in the hands of officers and a committee elected periodically (representative government and control of the cooperative);
h) A definite percentage of profits should be allotted to education (provision for education in cooperation);

i) Frequent statements and balance sheets should be presented to members (member information); and

j) No inquiry should be made into the political or religious opinions of those who apply for membership (political and religious neutrality) (Schaars, M.A. 1971: 69).

These Rochdalian rules were devised to run a small grocery store and although they have wide application, they are not necessarily appropriate for all types of cooperatives in all locations. Universally accepted Rochdale cooperative principles include the following:

a) Democratic control by member-users;

b) Limited dividends upon equity capital;

c) Operations at cost (with its corollary that if gross margins or incomes exceed costs, refunds will be made on patronage basis); and

d) Voluntary and open membership.

But the following are not adhered to by all associations:

a) Cash trading;

b) Charging prices that other dealers charge;

c) Sending out frequent statement and balance sheets; and

d) Setting aside a part of the new savings in an educational fund.

These rules have now been condensed into the following six principles: voluntary and open membership, democratic control, limited return on capital, surplus earnings belong to members, member education and co-operation among cooperatives (ICA, 1967; Melnyk, G. 1985: 3).

The success one might attribute to Rochdalians was by all means the shot in the arm that the cooperative movement needed in its doldrums days of the mid-eighteen forties. Rochdale became the beacon for others to follows. It was essentially a consumer's cooperative that sold household articles and food products to its members. Because of its success, it influenced the development of other cooperative organizations in other parts of the world.

Conclusion

The evolution of cooperative thought can be easily understood if we use the earliest permanent agrarian societies as a starting point. However, the industrial revolution had an impact in production and on the lives of people. There was development of new ideas that laid the foundation for modern cooperatives. Influential figures like Owen and his contemporaries, and the Rochdale pioneers in particular, contributed much to the creation of the principles, values and models of cooperatives.

References

Andrew, P., 1977, *Cooperative Institutions and Economic Development, Union of Manitoba, Canada,* Nairobi: East Africa Literature Bureau.

Digby, M, 1990, *World Co-operative Movement,* London: Hutchinso and Co. Ltd.

Holyoache, G.J., 1918, *The History of the Rochdale Pioneers,* New York: Charles Scriber's Sons.

International Cooperative Alliance, 1967, *Report of the International Cooperative Alliance Commission on Cooperative Principles,* London: International Co-operative Information Center.

Johnston, B., 1994, Co-operative: *The People's Business,* Manchester: Manchester University Press.

Krisha, M. M., 1972, *Cooperatives and Law,* Nairobi: East African Literature Bureau.

Lambert, P., 1963, *The Social Philosophy of Cooperation,* London: Manchester Cooperative Union.

Melnyk, G., 1985, *The Search for Community: From Utopia to a Cooperative Society,* Montreal-Buffalo: Black Rose Books.

Neal, P. S., 1981, *Cooperative and Development,* Madison: University of Wisconsin Press.

Prakash, D., 2003, *The Principles of Cooperation. A look at ICA Cooperative Identity Statement,* New Delhi: Rural Development and Management Centre.

Schaars, M. A., 1971, *Cooperatives, Principles and Practices,* Madison: University of Wisconsin Press.

Sharada, V., 1984, *The Theory of Co-operation,* Bombay: Himalaya Publishing House.

Young, C., Neal P.S. and Tim H. R., 1981, *Cooperative and Development Agricultural Politics in Ghana and Uganda,* Madison: *University of Wisconsin Press.*

3

The Theory of Peasant Cooperatives

This chapter examines the peasant economy according to Alexander Vasilevitch Chayanov and his theory of Peasant Cooperatives. Chayanov (1888-1937) was the major theorist of peasant studies in Russia. In the late 1920s he was regarded as an enemy of the State and was arrested in 1931 and executed in 1937. In 1987 he was officially rehabilitated and the importance of his ideas acknowledged.

In 1908, after his second year of study at the Moscow Agricultural Institute, 20 year-old Chayanov, spent his summer vacation in Italy and then in 1909 in Belgium. In both cases the time was used to study the work of cooperatives in the countryside and the agricultural services they provided (Danilov in Chayanov 1991: xxi). Chayanov developed a formulation for the main theme of his research: the model of the peasant economy. It is in his essays on Belgium that one can discern the starting point of his explanation of the importance of peasant cooperation.

Chayanov's initial analysis of the peasant economy was based on his populist ideas, so he conceptualized peasantry as a mode of production. His main objective was to show how to transform traditional rural society so as to overcome the misery, squalor and illiteracy of the peasantry and to show how peasants could modernize their agricultural practices, especially their farming techniques (Thornier, et. al 1991: xix).

3.1 Chanyanov's Model of the Peasant Economy

Chayanov's concept can be understood as a theory of the peasant mode of production at two levels: the level of labour process and the level of resource allocation, and examined the relationships peasants were engaged in during the course of their reproductive life. This is what he called "the labour consumer balance between the satisfaction of family needs and the drudgery of labour" (Chayanov, A.V, 1966: xv).

According to Chayanov, it is a misunderstanding to view the peasant family farm as a business- that is, an enterprise working to realize profit. This is because unlike the profit-oriented enterprise, peasant family farms were pure in the sense that they depended solely on the work of their own family members (Chayanov, A.V., 1966: xiii).

He worked on survey data collected from peasant farms in late the 19th and early 20th century in Russia and developed an economic model of the peasant family farm that did not use any wage labour. The data revealed that 90% or more of the farms in Russia in the first quarter of the 20th century had no hired labourers (Ibid: xiv). Because the peasant family farm lacked wage labour, it was impossible to work out the net gain, the rent and the interest on capital. He developed the model of peasant economy as a result. His model was concerned with the total income of the peasant family including off-farm earnings such as income from crafts and trade (Chayanov, A.V, 1966: xiv –v).

In developing his model, Chayanov began by examining the gross income in a peasant household at the end of an agricultural year. From this annual gross income certain expenses had to be deducted so as to restore the farm to the same level of production it possessed at the beginning of that agricultural year. These included seed, fodder, worn-out equipment and other inputs. After these expenses had been deducted, the family was left with a net income that constituted the return for its labour during that agricultural year (Ibid).

From Chayanov's conceptualization and analysis, the following can be deduced about the peasant economy:

First, the peasant economy involves intrinsic social relations that require the self-exploitation of labour power which can be measured by number of days in a year, during which the peasant chooses or is compelled to work on his/her farm; and

Second, the peasant economy reproduces itself through the family. It is the family that goes through a life cycle to drive an increase in the number of family members, hence population growth.

Chayanov identified the following key features of the peasant household economy:

a) In a peasant household economy, farm production was for use value and not for exchange;

b) In a peasant economy there was a commoditization of part of the family farm production in order to buy other use values like sugar, clothes or cooking oil which were not produced on the family farm;

c) Peasant economies were rural based;

d) The peasant economy was characterized by small scale units with less capital-intensive technologies than capitalist firms producing the same products;

e) That peasant farming predominantly relied on family labour showed how the demographic characteristics of the household determined the level of farm production; and

f) The peasant economy was characterized by homogeneous technology (Ennw, J., P. Hirst and K. Tribe, 1977: 248-249).

Chayanov developed his model by focusing on the pure family farm that employs no wage labour. Chayanov emphasized that peasant household income is derived from farm and non-farm sources. Thus, his model was developed primarily in terms of farm resource allocation (Chayanov 1966: 1).

Chayanov gave the following assumptions in his model of the peasant economy:

First, peasant households do not employ labour. They depend on family labour, hence the peasant economy does not involve wage payments, making it impossible to calculate profit using a capitalist formula.

Second, peasant households have entered into the sphere of monetary and commodity circulation. The demands which are not satisfied directly from farm production may be satisfied through purchases made. Thus trade and crafts are also essential features of the peasant economy (Chayanov 1966: 121-125).

Third, in each peasant family there is a socially determined minimum acceptable per capita income. This is determined by the demographic composition and size of the family. Thus the volume of economic activity (all forms of family economic activities such as in agriculture, crafts and trades) quantitatively corresponds to the basic elements of family composition. Therefore, the ratio between producer and consumers will determine the per capita income and the hours worked by the producers (Chayavov, 1966: 60). For any given farm, households with many producers would achieve higher output per producer because of the exploitation of the economies of scale in allocating labour time (some in farming, others in trade, crafts, domestic work, livestock etc.).

Fourth, land is in flexible supply to all households and this can be through rent or communal repartition. However, Chayanov noted that there is the possibility of limits to land supply. And if this happens, peasants will adjust their resource allocation by increasing the intensity of exploitation of existing land or by increasing off-farm work (Chayanov, 1966: 111-112). Intensification can be in the form of mixed cropping and increased off-farm work.

Fifth, in peasant households, production takes place up to the point where the marginal utility of output is equal to the marginal disutility of work. This is to say that peasants produce to meet their desired level of satisfaction which is primarily subsistence and not beyond that. Thus income per capita (over any given time period) beyond the socially acceptable minimum has diminishing marginal utility (Ibid.).

Sixth, managerial skills involved in production do not vary significantly between households: they are more or less the same.

Seventh, capital may be obtained through farm income accumulation or from borrowing from banks (Chayanov, 1966: 111-112).

3.2 Criticism of Chayanov's Model of the Peasant Economy

A number of criticisms have been directed against Chayanov's model of the peasant economy, particularly by Marxist scholars. Harrison (1975, 1977) wrote from a Marxist perspective. His criticisms were directed against Chayanov's explanation of economic differentiation. His criticisms focused on Chayanov's assumptions, his interpretation of empirical evidence, and some propositions derived from his assumptions and interpretations.

First, the data used by Chayanov provided weak support for the trend that low producer and consumer ratios cause low levels of per capital income and expenditure. This depended on the technology used. For example, a family with five people where three people are producers and they use a plough to cultivate, given good climatic conditions: their per capita income may be high. But the expenditure is not only influenced by the size of the family. Other behaviors of household members such as the farmer being an alcoholic who sells the farm produce not only to fulfill the family's needs but also to meet his desire for alcohol consumption.

Second, Chayanov defined family farms as production units which depended on family labour. He assumed that 90 per cent of farms in Russia in the first quarter of the twentieth century had no hired labour. This ignored the heterogeneous nature of farm owners. (poor, middle class and rich farmers). For example, there were a number of people in rural areas who depended on wage labour to earn their living. The wage labourers were normally hired by middle class and rich farmers.

Third, Chayanov failed to identify the distinction between the economic conditions faced by poor peasants and rich farmers. He did not take into account the fact that rich farmers and poor peasants faced different conditions. Rich farmers had favourable conditions in terms of prices for their farm inputs and farm outputs (as they may have been of a large quantity and of a higher quality). Also Chayanov did not capture the involuntary unemployment of poor farmers caused by lack of access to resources and the voluntary idleness of rich farmers due to their ability to hire wage labour.

Harrison (1977) claimed that the capital accumulation of peasants had not been that much easier because of unreliable climatic conditions, low prices for their crops, higher rents and lower yields on rented land. Poor peasants also paid high prices for farm inputs and had diminishing returns on their labour and therefore they found it difficult to accumulate capital.

Neo-Marxists criticized the model of peasant economy because it ignored the extent of the external relationship with the capitalist economy. The model neither considered the attempts of rich farmers to expand by using wage employment and using farm capital nor the constraints regarding access to land and other resources which affected poor peasants.

Chayanov has also been criticized for ignoring changes that might have taken place in society, for instance, the increase in population, which would automatically lead to the division of labour and specialization. As a result, stratification took place with the emergence of poor and rich farmers.

3.3 Chayanov's Theory of Peasant Cooperatives

3.3.1 *Ideas on Peasant Cooperatives*

Chayanov was not only concerned with peasant agriculture but also with the theory of cooperatives. Basic ideas on peasant cooperatives were founded on experience in the cooperative movements in Russia. He believed that through cooperatives, which entailed the amalgamation of meager resources, peasants would increase their production. He maintained that the horizontal concentration of production offered only limited advantages in agriculture, as the studies of farm sizes showed. On the other hand, vertical concentration allowed agriculture to achieve a revolution comparable to that of the steam engine industry (Chayanov A.V, 1966: xvii).

Chayanov had the view that through integration of agriculture through cooperatives an agricultural revolution would be possible. This would lead to intensive and extensive cultivation through the use of modern agro-inputs such as tractors, and fertilizers, etc. as well as improvements in livestock breeding.

3.3.2 *Theory of the Peasant Cooperative*

Chayanov thought that the cooperative of the future would bring the possibility of protecting small-scale peasant households under conditions of market competition and through the economic and social merits of cooperation. Chayanov saw the advantages which peasants would get through cooperatives in market specialization and in the use of complex machinery and in the achievements of science.

Chayanov considered that the very nature of an agricultural enterprise placed limits on the enlargement in terms of its scale and therefore, the advantages of a large-scale over a small-scale economy in agriculture could never be very great in quantitative terms. Practical experience led him to the conclusion that cooperation had the capacity to impart all the advantages of a large-scale economy to small-scale peasant households (Danilov in Chayanov 1991: xxvii – xxviii). Small-scale peasant households, when joined in cooperative association, achieve a scale and potential that is actually greater than those of the private farms.

The comparison between small-scale and large-scale farms was not confined to the sphere of production. Chayanov also analyzed the social differences. We have to compare a farm which is operated by its owner and by the manpower of the owner's family on the one hand, and a capitalist farm which is operated by hired labour on the other. For Chayanov, peasant households could benefit from advantages realized to their full extent under conditions of a cooperative system. Under those conditions, the path was opened to constant intensification of labour, the growth of production and social wealth combined with a guarantee to democratize the distribution of the income from cooperative enterprise.

Chayanov provided a concrete picture of the organization and functioning of various forms of agricultural cooperation and of all the main branches of their work and provided validation for the concept of the cooperative peasant economy. The cooperative peasant economy was part of the peasant economy which had been split off for the purpose of being organized on large-scale principles. Cooperation would exist for as long as the peasant economy existed; and it was this which predetermined the limits of cooperative collectivization (Chayanov, 1927).

The idea of 'cooperative collectivization' was endorsed in V.I. Lenin's article 'On Cooperation' written in 1923 particularly in his conclusion that for the Russian peasants, the growth of cooperation was in itself identical to the growth of socialism. This would abolish private ownership of land and create cooperative farms.

Chayanov analyzed the 'horizontal' and 'vertical' type of concentration of production in depth, dealing with their potential and their interrelationship (Chayanov, 1927). There is a powerful upsurge of production, accompanied by social progress along the path of 'vertical concentration', that is, the growing diversity and interaction between different farms and scales of organizing production processes and in economic ties of both the cooperative and the non-cooperative varieties. Vertical concentration involved the use of science and modern technology in farm production.

By contrast, production would stagnate and there will be a social stalemate if the path of 'horizontal concentration' was followed. This involved merging farms to create larger farms. From the point of view of socialist development, 'vertical integration' in its cooperative form was obviously preferred.

Chayanov (1927) indicated how in the long term the establishment of a cooperative system of agricultural production meant that the entire system underwent a qualitative transformation. This transformation from a system of peasant households where cooperation covered certain branches of the economy into a system based on a public cooperative rural economy. The latter system was built on the foundation being the socialization of capital which leaves the implementation of certain processes to the private households of its members.

'Horizontal concentration' in the form of collective farms was in no way rejected out of hand. Collective farms, set up by peasants of their own free will, on their own initiative, and in their own interests could and should be part of the cooperative system in accordance with general cooperative principles, Chayanov wrote: "The choice would not be between collectives and cooperatives. The essence of the choice would be whether the membership of cooperatives is to be drawn from collectives or from the peasant family households." (Chayanov, 1991: 205).

Chayanov believed that 'Cooperative collectivization' represented the best and perhaps the only possible way of introducing to the peasant economy elements of a large-scale economy, of industrialization, and of state planning (Chayanov, 1991: 21). What he saw as its merit was that it could be implemented on an entirely voluntary and economic basis which amounted to 'self collectivization.' The idea of 'cooperative collectivization' was a reflection of the basic tendency of the actual development of cooperation in the Russian countryside in the 1920s and offered a real alternative to forced collectivization of the Stalinist variety.

Cooperation could combine the advantages of small peasant properties and the technical advantages of large-scale farming. Chayanov saw the possibility of agricultural transformation when peasants used science and technology. However, this was not possible to apply to an individual peasant but, through cooperatives, the use of new methods and equipment would be possible.

Chayanov believed that technical transformation could grow from an indigenous technology to a modern technology. He thought that each peasant had talents spread among the different farm practices such as planting, weeding, harvesting and livestock keeping and if these talents joined together through cooperatives, the peasant economy would grow. He also said that through cooperatives, peasants would be able to sell farm products jointly and that would give them the opportunity to bargain for higher prices for their farm products instead of selling their products individually and in small quantities.

Chayanov identified the following features of cooperatives:

First, a cooperative is a voluntary organization and a member can join or quit at any time at will. There is no forced cooperative membership.

Second, a cooperative should be controlled democratically. No member has more say than others. Decisions are made democratically through voting on the basis one-member one-vote.

Third, membership in a cooperative is open and there is no restriction to membership based on ideological, religious or political views. Membership restriction based on these factors would weaken cooperatives on open membership.

Chayanov's theory on cooperatives is relevant to Tanzania. 80% of the Tanzanian population lives in rural areas as peasants. They mostly use poor farming technology, particularly hand hoes, and they do not employ modern, scientific agricultural methods. Thus the ideas of Chayanov to modernize agriculture are a point of focus in transforming peasant agriculture systems based on cooperatives, which would make it feasible for peasant access to agro-inputs, which include fertilizers, tractors/ploughs, quality seeds and good animal breeding methods and pesticides.

The cooperative theory developed by Chayanov is relevant in that cooperatives could help to overcome social difficulties that inevitably accompany economic modernization (Maghimbi, S 1990: 92).

Vertical concentration of production allowed agriculture to achieve a revolution. The whole point of this vertical intergration was to reconcile the maintenance of peasant farms in the process of intensive cultivation and livestock breeding, which included the requirement of technical progress whereas the large enterprise had an advantage in mechanization, production and marketing. The agricultural cooperative was to be the instrument of that integration. Chayanov also insisted that the main form of peasant farm concentration can only be done vertically in its cooperative form since it was the only way to be organically linked with agricultural production and able to spread to its proper extent and depth. Chayanov believed that through cooperatives it is possible to amalgamate the limited resources of peasants and make it possible to increase peasant production. He believed that vertical integration of agriculture could be achieved through cooperatives.

Further more, Chayanov saw advantages of cooperatives, with their potential to make peasants adopt new agricultural methods. Also, resources could be made available through cooperative organizations. Technical transformations were possible through peasant cooperatives because cooperative organizations could mobilize people to adopt new technical methods in farming. Also, there was a possibility to expand the marketing of farm products through cooperatives according to needs that are both internal and external. Finally cooperatives were a source of change as, according to Chayanov, cooperatives could strengthen social, economic, and cultural changes.

Chayanov was criticized by the state in Russia for rejecting the creation of Stalinist-type collectivization, which had limited advantages in agriculture and insisting on vertical concentration, which leads to agricultural revolution. He also rejected the communization of production and insisted on labour incentives, organization of labour, and managerial will.

References

Akpoghor, P.S., 1993, *Selected Essays on Cooperation Theory and Practice,* Murburg: Murburg Consult for self help Promotion.

Chayanov, A. V., 1991, *The Theory of Peasant Cooperatives,* London: Tauris and Co. Ltd.

Chayanov, A.V., 1927, *The Basic Ideas and Organizational Forms of Agricultural Cooperation,* Second Edition, Revised and Supplemented, Moscow: Shanyavkii University Publishing House.

Chayanov, A.V., 1966, *The Theory of Peasant Economy,* Illinois: Homewood.

Chayanov, A.V., 1991, *The Theory of Peasant Econom,*. Thorner D., B. Kerblay and R.E.G. Smith. (eds.), London: Tauris and Co. Ltd.

Ennew, Judith, Paul Hirst and Keith Tribe, 1977, 'Peasantry as an Economic Category', *Journal of Peasant Studies,* 4, 4: 295 – 322.

Forster, P.G. and Maghimbi, S., (eds.), 1999, *Agrarian Economy, State and Society in Contemporary Tanzania,* Aldershot: Ashgate Publishing Ltd.

Foster, P.G. and S. Maghimbi (eds.), 1992, *The Tanzania Peasantry: Economy in Crisis,* Aldershot: Ashgate Publishing Ltd.

Harrison, Mark, 1977, 'The Peasant Mode of Production in the Work of A.V. Chayanov', in *Journal of Peasant Studies,* 4, 4: 323-336.

Hunt, Diana, 1977, 'Chayanov's Model of Peasant Household Resource Allocation' in *Journal of Peasant Studies,* 6, 3: 247-285.

Lenin, V.I., 1923, *On Cooperation,* Moscow: Progress Publishers.

Maghimbi, S., 1990, 'Cooperatives in Agricultural Development' in O'Neill, N. and Mustafa, K. (eds.), 1990, *Capitalism, Socialism and Development Crisis in Tanzania,* Aldershot: Avebury, pp. 81-100.

Melnyls, G., 1985, *The Search for Community: From Utopian to a Cooperative Society,* Montreal – Buffalo: Black Rose Books.

Thorner, D., B. Kerblay and R.E.G. Smith (eds.), 1991, *The Theory of Peasant Economy,* London: Tauris and Co. Ltd.

4

The Rise of Cooperatives in Tanzania

During the pre-colonial period people worked together because they had long since learned it was the best way to solve the problems that lay beyond individual reach and to achieve maximum benefits for the group. They hunted together; they helped one another built shelters, and so on. As a group, it was possible to make use of varied individual talents and skills for the benefit of all members.

This chapter analyzes the struggle of peasants against middle men and the colonial state. The colonial economy, the African peasantry, and Asian middle men are examined in connection with the rise of farmers' crop marketing cooperatives. The chapter presents landmarks in the development of agricultural cooperatives[2] in Tanzania. In the analysis the focus is placed on three aspects: firstly, the cooperative movement since the early 1930's; secondly, the role and success of agricultural cooperatives under the socio-economic conditions of Tanganyika; and thirdly, the identification of some problems and challenges which the agricultural cooperatives in Tanzania encountered during the colonial administration in Tanganyika (Tanzanian mainland)[3].

During the Berlin conference (1884/1885) it was decided how to divide Africa among Imperialist nations, and Tanganyika fell under German rule. The Germans opened their colonial project with the German East African Company, which failed, but then continued it in 1896 with direct rule following the installation of a satellite German government. Tanganyika came under British colonial rule after the First World War, and it became a mandated territory of the League of Nations.

4.1 The Colonial State and the Colonial Economy

During British rule over Tanganyika, the colonial economy had the following economic categories:

a) Large and medium-scale European plantations, estates and settler farms growing coffee, sisal, etc.

b) Smallholder African export cash-crops such as coffee, cotton, tea, tobacco, cashew nuts, cloves and copra. The export crops contributed to the biggest proportion of the total Gross Domestic Product (GDP). The colonial economy was export oriented. There was uneven development in rural areas, which was further fostered by colonial policy:

2 According to the cooperative principles of the International Cooperative Alliance, cooperatives are formal self-help business organizations. (Abrahamsen, 1976: 53).

3 Tanzania is a union of Tanganyika and Zanzibar which came into being in 1964. This study deals with the cooperative movement on the Tanzania mainland (Tanganyika).

(i) Some areas were ear-marked to grow export crops, eg. Kilimanjaro (coffee, sisal), Tanga (sisal), Bukoba (coffee), Mbeya (coffee, tea); Zanzibar and Pemba (cloves, coconuts), Mwanza and Mara (cotton); and

(ii) Some areas were labour reservoirs that provided labourers who worked in other areas with export cash crops, eg. on sisal estates, coffee plantations or in mines, public works, etc. These areas included Ruvuma, Kigoma, Tabora and Rukwa.

This division served the colonial economy but was not thorough-going and complete because of the following factors:

a) In cash crop growing areas, food production was necessary because the monetary and real value of crops sold by smallholders could not cover their subsistence needs, thus cash crop farming had to be complemented by growing staples such as bananas and legumes in the coffee growing areas;

b) In labour-reservoir areas, the migrant labourers could not meet their subsistence needs through the meager wages paid so their families had to produce food crops to supplement the wages; and

c) The colonial state introduced taxes (head tax, hut tax, cattle tax) in peasant areas, and as a result peasants were forced to grow cash crops or to sell labour power to earn money to pay the taxes (Cliffe, L. et al. (editors) 1975).

Thus by way of state intervention-both purposefully and spontaneously through market or exchange activities-all areas found themselves enmeshed in the colonial economy as producers of crops for sale or as labourers.

The paramount objective of the colonial state was to maintain law and order and supervise and regulate the economy. Economic activities enabled the metropolitan bourgeoisie to obtain cheap raw materials for their industries, cheap labour for the extraction of surplus, and monopoly markets where manufactured commodities from the metropolitan industries could be sold. The colonial state allowed and assisted private Asian middlemen to buy agricultural produce which was subsequently sold to import/export houses in Britain. The exploitative colonial structure also permitted various intermediary agents to purchase and market farm products and to supply credit at high interest rates and inputs at high prices. These agents played a significant role in the vertical integration of cash-crop production and marketing.

There were social and economic discontents which arose among crop producers because of the exploitative colonial arrangements. These grievances among cash crops producers led to the establishment of farmers' cooperatives for marketing farm products. The colonial government enacted laws to register cooperatives in order to regulate and control them. An alternative option would have been to ignore the demands of the producers. This could have increased the costs of colonial administration in order to coerce peasants' acquiescence to the system of exploitation or it could have politicized the peasants to the point of radicalization, which would have threatened the colonial economy.

The colonial state allowed and supported cooperative development because its producers were numerous smallholders and cooperatives made it possible for economies of scale in the input of supplies and handling, and in the marketing of agricultural products through cooperatives. Cooperatives performed bulk handling of products and reduced the cost per unit of products which were marketed through them.

4.2 African Peasantry and Traders

The African peasantry was characterized by smallholders. These were peasants with farms that were relatively small, many from 0.5 to 3 hectares and they were managed with family labour and in some cases by mutual aid through kinship or the extended family. Earnings from such smallholdings, both in monetary (exchange value) and real terms (use values) were mainly sufficient to meet subsistence needs. Smallholders mainly used traditional means to cultivate, such as hand hoes and in some cases ox-drawn ploughs.

The introduction of cash-crop production brought about the stratification of the peasantry as rich, middle and poor peasants, and rural labourers. There were cases whereby rich rural producers moved away from farm productive activities to become petty retail traders and facilitated the exchanges between rural traders. African petty traders could not evolve fully into capitalist traders because of deliberate colonial policy, which in the economic realm purposely encouraged the division of labour and specialization on racial and ethnic grounds.

Asian traders were given credit facilities to conduct business. These traders were encouraged to play an intermediary role. Most Asians, except for those on the large sisal estates or other large-scale farms, could not acquire land for smallholdings to cultivate. On the other hand, there were laws that specifically set low limits to the amount of credit an African trader could receive. These factors led to united actions among Africans (peasants and traders) to organize and manage agricultural marketing cooperatives. The analysis in this context leads us to understand the dynamics and motives for the development of cooperatives. The objectives, functions and modes of operation of cooperatives were consistent with the interest of the people they served.

Coffee growing was introduced by Roman Catholic missionaries in Kilema and became a popular cash crop among Chagga farmers dwelling on the slopes of Mount Kilimanjaro in the 1920s. All coffee grown by Chagga farmers was sold through Asian and European middlemen who dealt directly with buyers outside the country. As was the case in such situations, the middlemen, who enjoyed tremendous government support, used their positions of influence to exploit the farmers in all possible ways. There were no acceptable measures to determine the quality and grade of crops sold and this gave way to peasants being cheated when their products were priced. Even after introducing weighing scales, the level of illiteracy among most peasants was a factor that allowed Asian middlemen to continue exploiting them. They used various tricks to maneuver weighing scales and to falsify grading to justify lower payments for the coffee they bought (Kimario 1992: 3).

Peasants grew very suspicious of the marketing system and sent complaints to their chiefs, who forwarded their grievances to the colonial government. The peasants believed that Asian merchants were agents of the colonial bourgeoisie and were there to exploit them. This led to great discontent. On their own initiative, African peasants established their own associations. This was an effort to improve their position against the middlemen.

4.3 Conditions for the Formation of Cooperatives

Favorable conditions for the formation of cooperatives developed as peasants cultivating cash crops- coffee, cotton, and tobacco- wanted better marketing conditions for their produce. Cash-crop farming took place where climate and soil conditions were favorable. These included areas such as Kilimanjaro, Meru, Arusha, Mwanza, Bukoba, and the Southern Highlands, where good rainfall could sustain cash cropping. The colonial government encouraged cash-crop farming to supply exports for overseas markets. African farmers were encouraged to grow crops by the following factors:

a) Surplus labour and availability of land were important factors in cash-crop farming.

b) Availability of reliable transport, especially railway and road transport, enabled farmers to transport their crops to the processing plants and for export;

c) Entrepreneurship among Africans who had attained some education and trading knowledge organized peasants to market farm products; and

d) Policies of the colonial government– taxes were imposed, forcing people to cultivate cash crops or sell labour power.

Cooperative societies were, first and foremost established in cash-crop areas, such as the coffee growing areas of Kilimanjaro, Bukoba, and Tukuyu and in cotton growing areas which included the Lake Victoria Zone and Sukuma Land. Farmers believed that the prices paid for their crops were too low. They also believed that Asian middlemen were exploiting them by dishonestly weighing crops. Peasants believed that by joining to form associations they could eliminate Asian exploitation. Cooperatives in Tanganyika were also struggling against attempts by European settlers to have a monopoly over coffee production in Kilimanjaro.

4.4 Peasant Cooperatives During the Colonial Administration

During the British colonial administration, agricultural marketing cooperatives were first started in cash-crop farming areas. Peasants saw advantages to joint efforts in marketing their crops. The benefits of handling and selling together became obvious to cash crop growers. The colonial administration saw marketing cooperatives as convenient institutions for the colonial economy because Asian middlemen were sometimes unreliable in cases where they considered an enterprise to be unprofitable to them. Marketing cooperatives were a reliable institution to buy crops from peasants, so the colonial government intervened through laws and regulations regarding cooperatives and crop marketing. By using crop prices and farm credits, the administration regulated the production of the cash crops which were channeled to markets through cooperatives.

In 1925, Kilimanjaro African coffee growers organized themselves and formed the first farmers' association in Tanganyika. This was the Kilimanjaro Native Planters' Association (KNPA) which was formed under Joseph Merinyo. This was a voluntary association which helped

African coffee growers to organize their coffee farming. The expansion of coffee production among the Chagga faced strong opposition from the Europeans settlers who did everything in their power to maintain a monopoly over the crop (Kimario 1992: 2). The KNPA protected peasants from opposition by the European coffee planters, who thought that the development of coffee farming by Africans was a threat to both the quality of Kilimanjaro coffee and the supply of African labour power. By 1926, the KNPA was operating and it performed the following functions:

a) To protect and promote the interest of indigenous coffee growers;
b) To assist in proper control of coffee planting and guard against pests and diseases;
c) To assist in the sale of products at the highest possible price; and
d) To supply fertilizers and necessary equipment for the improvement of the coffee industry (Kimario, A 1992: 4).

Although the association performed these functions it faced huge problems caused by the world economic depression of the 1930s. Low prices for coffee in the world market and adverse propaganda spread by settlers and middlemen against the KNPA led to the collapse of the association. European coffee farmers had previously organized themselves under the Tanganyika Coffee Growers' Association (TCGA), combining over their mutual interest regarding the following concerns against African smallholders:

a) The demand that Africans should not be allowed to produce coffee because they were ignorant about coffee husbandry and would threaten to adulterate coffee by bringing in plant diseases;
b) To allow Africans to grow coffee would bring about a shortage of labourers for the large coffee estates of settlers who were dependent on the supply of cheap native labour; and
c) The settlers wanted further alienation of land. (Kimario 1992).

The colonial state supported smallholders to continue growing coffee and also to organize the marketing of their products by providing services related to farm input supplie. To support and assist African coffee growers, the colonial government also enacted the Cooperative Societies Ordinance. In 1931 Mr. C.F Strickland, a Registrar of Cooperatives in Punjab, India came to Tanganyika to advise the government on how to promote cooperatives and to determine appropriate legislation which would allow their growth. The Cooperative legislations, which were based on The Indian Acts of 1904 and 1912 (modified slightly by the laws in Sri Lanka and Ghana), were embodied in the Cooperative Societies Ordinance of March 1932 (Kimario 1992: 4-5).

The Cooperative Societies Ordinance of 1932 authorized the establishment and registration of cooperative societies in Tanganyika. (Ngeze, 1975: 8, and Strickland, 1933). The Ordinance defined cooperatives as institutions with voluntary memberships, organized and run democratically to carry out business enterprise for the benefit of their members. The governor appointed a Registrar of Cooperatives in 1932 to conduct the registration and supervision of cooperatives.

The government dissolved the KNPA and it was re-registered it as a cooperative under the name of the Kilimanjaro Native Cooperative Union Ltd. (KNCU) in 1933. Its 11 affiliated primary societies were also registered. The main objectives of the primary societies were:

a) To provide marketing services required before crop produce was delivered to KNCU for marketing;

b) To provide all necessary assistance and guidance to members, to prevent and eradicate pests and disease likely to affect their crops;

c) To advance loans to members on security of their products; and

d) To encourage the spirit and practices of thrift and mutual self-help among its members.

The KNCU. and its affiliated primary societies became the first marketing cooperatives in Tanzania (Muungano wa vyama vya Ushirika, 1977: 5). In 1937, the government enacted an ordinance which gave the governor power to establish native coffee boards in Tanzania. These boards were not cooperatives but were given powers to see that all African coffee growers in a specific area sold their coffee through the board or through such agencies as the board might direct. In the same year, the Moshi Native Coffee Board was established and the board appointed the KNCU. to be its agent for the purchase of coffee from the Kilimanjaro African Coffee Growers. The board was later dissolved and its functions taken over by the KNCU. because it was successful in buying coffee produce.

During the colonial period, the cooperative movement spread to other cash-crop farming areas. Exploitation by Asian middlemen in the marketing of African cash crops was an important grievance which provided the motivation to establish early marketing cooperatives (Saul,

1973: 142). In the Songea district, the Ngoni-Matengo Cooperative Union Ltd. (NGOMAT) was registered in 1936 with its three affiliated primary societies for marketing tobacco. In the same year the Bugufi Coffee Cooperative Union Ltd. in Ngara district was registered with its five affiliated primary societies (Ngeze, 1975: 13) to market coffee crops for its members, to educate them on how to improve coffee farming, and to supply them with farm inputs.

After the Second World War, more Africans embarked on cash-crop farming for export and the cooperative movement spread faster. In 1947, coffee growers in the Rungwe district established the Mwakaleli Coffee Growers Cooperative Society, a forerunner to the Rungwe African Cooperative Union Ltd. (RACU) which was registered in 1949 with its 10 affiliated primary societies (Ngeze, 1975: 16). The primary societies included five paddy-marketing societies until 1958, when they separated to form the Unyakyusa Cooperative Union Ltd. Coffee growers in the Bukoba district established the Bukoba Native Cooperative Union Ltd. (BNCU) which was registered with its 48 affiliated primary societies in 1950. Meru coffee growers started the Koimere African Cooperative Society, which was registered in 1949.

Among cotton growers, the Lake Province Growers Association in Mwanza was established in 1949. Later, cotton farmers started their own marketing cooperatives. In 1955, this cotton zone had 113 cotton marketing cooperative primary societies which were affiliated to 9 cotton cooperative unions. In the same year, these unions formed the Victoria Federation of Cooperative Unions (VFCU). By 1960 the VFCU, which later became the Nyanza Cooperative Union Ltd. (NCU), had 360 primary societies, making it the largest cooperative in Africa (Ngeze, 1975: 18). These cooperatives marketed their members' cotton to avoid exploitation by Asian middlemen (Maguire, 1969: 126; Hyden, 1976: 10).

Other agricultural cooperatives which were started in 1960 were the Morogoro Cooperative Union Ltd. with 20 affiliated primary societies for marketing paddy, the Mbozi African Cooperative Union Ltd. with seven affiliated societies for marketing coffee and the Usambara Cooperative Union Ltd. with seven affiliated societies for marketing coffee. By the end of 1960, Tanzania had a total of 30 marketing cooperative unions and 691 cooperative primary societies (Cooperative Development Division, 1969: 1).

The colonial government in Tanganyika allowed for the development of crop marketing cooperatives to ensure a smooth flow of crops to the colonial metropolitan industries. The marketing cooperatives also enabled African cash crop growers to strengthen their bargaining position. Agricultural cooperatives also distributed farm inputs. But the low level of socio-economic development which existed in Tanganyika was an obstacle to the growth of the cooperative movement. The low level of education left a shortage of adequately-trained staff in cooperatives. Some cooperative members lacked even the basic tools of literacy, which are vital for the genuine control of a cooperative by its members.

4.5 How Cooperatives Operated in Tanganyika During the British Colonial Administration

Cooperatives in Tanganyika operated hand in hand with the building of stores for storage of agricultural produce including warehouses and granaries throughout the country. The colonial government was responsible for ensuring the construction of such storage buildings and infrastructural bases in the productive areas. It also provided subsidies to farmers' cooperatives for agro-inputs such as pesticides, fertilizers, and seeds. In all cooperative societies in Tanganyika, market prices for farm products were strictly arranged and determined by the colonial government, while peasants had no say in the matter.

Cooperative operations in rural areas went hand in hand with the provision of extension services and cooperative education to farmers in topics such as the use of seeds, fertilizers, crop spacing, and spraying. Marketing cooperatives were responsible for farm husbandry, purchasing quality farm products, selling products, and paying members good prices on product sales. Cooperatives brought the vertical integration of peasants into the monetary economy. As agents of modernization, cooperatives brought poor peasants more firmly into the monetary economy.

At the time of Independence in 1961, the cooperative movement had achieved a remarkable level of growth in terms of both membership and volume of business. In 1961, cooperative societies consisted of 739 crop marketing, 4 mining, 4 savings and credit, 10 consumer and 3 transport cooperatives. The cooperative movement emerged as the biggest African-owned and managed business organization in Tanganyika.

The main objective for the formation of cooperatives during the colonial administration was to fight against exploitation of native cash crop growers by Asian and European middlemen- exploitation which was buttressed by the colonial government. In this regard, cooperatives helped in the marketing and in the provision of services in order to make native cash crop growers deliver products that were competitive in the market. Apart from this main objective, there were specific objectives for each cooperative union (Kimario, 1992). For example, Kilimanjaro Native Cooperative Union (KNCU.) had the following objectives:

a) To market all coffee grown by indigenous farmers on behalf of its affiliated societies;

b) To purchase supplies for members (such as seeds, agricultural and building materials) in bulk in order to reap the benefit of large-scale operations (bulk wholesale prices);

c) To provide loans to affiliated societies according to the stipulated law;

d) To exercise regular and careful inspection and supervision of affiliated society accounts;

e) To secure loans from financial institutions such as banks to advance its objectives;

f) To receive and invest deposits from affiliated societies and their members; and

g) Lastly, to promote the spirit and practice of thrift and mutual self-help (Kimario, 1992: 5-6).

The Tanganyika Cooperative Trading Agency (TACTA) was established in 1952 in response to the disadvantaged position of weaker coffee cooperative unions. It was intended to assist member unions to market their coffee more efficiently, to provide members with insurance services and also to supply its members with farm implements and other essential farm requirements. Cooperatives which benefited from TACTA services were The Bugufi Cooperatives Union of Ngara district and the Rungwe African Cooperative Union of Rungwe, Mbeya (Kimario, 1992: 12-13).

4.6 Cooperative Achievements During the Colonial Administration

Cooperatives helped to reduce exploitation by Asian and European middlemen. They helped in the search for markets for native growers' crops and the provision of necessary inputs in order to improve farm production for better yields (Kimario, 1992).

In 1957, it was agreed in the general meeting of the Bukoba Native Cooperative Union Ltd. (BNCU) to establish an educational fund created through a special levy of half a cent for every pound of coffee delivered to societies. The fund was used to build schools and sponsor members' children to study in local schools or abroad (Kimario, 1992: 9). BNCU was also able to establish its own cooperative schools at Maruku, Gera, and Igabiro where regular seminars and courses for committee members and staff were conducted. BNCU owned a bi-monthly newspaper, the Buhaya Cooperative News, launched to inform its members about cooperation and to highlight problems that local cooperatives faced in their endeavor to achieve their set objectives. The Union also operated a hotel, the Coffee Tree Inn (Kimario, 1992: 9).

Another cooperative which had marks of success was Kilimanjaro Native cooperative Union Ltd. Throughout its history KNCU played a key role in improving the social and economic welfare of coffee farmers living on the slopes of Mount Kilimanjaro. Its contribution to their development included the establishment of schools, a college, a public library, health centers, restaurants, etc. The union also served as a model for other cooperatives in the country. In this case, it was possible for farmers and cooperators from other parts of the country to learn from the experience which KNCU had accumulated over the years (Kimario, 1992: 7).

The Meru Cooperative Union (M.C.U.) also had good achievements. This union established seedling beds and a demonstration farm, supplied fertilizers, insecticides, and equipment for spraying and hand pulping machines. M.C.U. also provided a savings and credit scheme to its members (Kimario, 1992: 15).

The birth of the Tanganyika African National Union (TANU.) in 1954 marked the beginning of widespread political mobilization of people for political independence. TANU was a nationalist party fighting for the independence of Tanganyika. The struggle was not only directed against the colonial government but also against middlemen who amassed wealth at the expense of farmers. Farmers' cooperatives were part and parcel to the struggle for independence (Kimario, 1992: 18).

4.7 Problems and Challenges that Faced Cooperatives During Colonial Rule

Marketing cooperatives faced numerous challenges and problems. The Kilimanjaro Native Cooperative Union, for example, was faced with the problem of low coffee prices. From 1935 to 1942, the price of coffee remained almost stagnant, at the same low level of between 35 and 40 sterling pounds per tonne. This situation had disastrous effects on the morale of cooperative members who did not know the connection between the world economic depression and crop prices paid by their cooperatives.

The government promulgated a series of laws which made it compulsory for Chagga farmers to sell their coffee through the established cooperatives. This measure made the farmers feel that the KNCU. had become a government-owned organization rather than being owned by them. The KNCU. faced opposition from its members. In 1937, the ensuing riots had a devastating effect on KNCU. property but the situation was quickly controlled by the government (Kimario, 1992: 6).

The Meru Cooperative Union encountered serious problems from European settlers and Asian middlemen. The Europeans tried to discourage African farmers from expanding their coffee production because of the same fears which had been expressed by their counterparts in Kilimanjaro. The Asian middlemen, on the other hand, used all sorts of tricks to ensure that they got profits from coffee proceeds (Kimario, 1992: 14).

Conclusion

At independence in 1961, the cooperative movement had achieved a remarkable pace of growth both in membership and in volume of business. Marketing cooperatives were basically established by African cash crop farmers to market their produce and overcome the exploitation of Asian and European middlemen who were buying the crops. Cooperatives also sold agro-inputs to farmers and supplied farm services to African crop producers. Cooperatives united the native coffee growers against the European opposition to African coffee growers and overcame the European monopoly in coffee marketing. On the other hand the colonial government passed a Cooperative ordinance in 1932 to register and supervises Cooperatives to ensure that they contributed to the colonial economy in supplying raw materials to British industries. Due to the expansion of the cooperative movement, the government sponsored most of the cooperative department staff to study at the East African School of Cooperation in Kabete, Kenya and the Cooperative College in Loughborough, Britain. Another School of Cooperation was opened at Mzumbe in 1957 for training cooperative staff.

References

Cliff, L. Peter Lawrence, William Luttrell, Shem Migot-Adholla and John S. Saul (eds.), 1975, *Rural Cooperation in Tanzania,* Dar es Salaam: Tanzania Publishing House.

Cooperative Development Division, 1969, *Notes on Cooperative Movement in Tanzania,* Dar es Salaam: Government Printer.

Dimoso, A., 1993, The Impact of Policy Changes on the Cooperative Movement in Tanzania, University of Dar es Salaam, Dissertation.

Hyden G., 1973, *East Africa Cooperatives: A Study of Organizational Conflicts,* Uppasala: East African Studies.

Hyden, G., (ed), 1976, *Cooperatives in Tanzania: Problems of Organization Building,* Dar es Salaam: Tanzania Publishing House Ltd.

Kimario, A.M., 1992, *Marketing Cooperatives in Tanzania: Problems and Prospects,* Dar es Salaam: Dar es Salaam University Press.

Krishan M, 1972, *Cooperatives and Law,* Nairobi: East African Literature Bureau.

Maguire, A.G., 1969, *Toward Uhuru in Tanzania: The Politics of Participation,* London: Cambridge University Press.

Muungano wa Vyama vya Ushirika Tanganyika, 1977, *Ushirika Wetu*, Dar es Salaam: Printfast.

Ngeze. P., 1975, *Ushirika Tanzania,* Dar es Salaam: Tanzania Publishing House Ltd.

Saul, J.S., 1973, 'Marketing Cooperatives in a Developing country – The Tanzania Case.' In Cliffe, L. and John S. Saul (eds.), 1973, *Socialism in Tanzania: Policies, An Interdisciplinary Reader,* 2, 54, Dar es Salaam: East African Publishing House.

Schaarrs, M.A., 1973, *Cooperatives, Principles and Practices,* Madison: University of Wisconsin Press.

Sharada, V., 1986, *The Theory of Cooperation,* Bombay: Himalaya Publishing House.

Strickland C. F., 1933, *Cooperation for Africa,* London: Oxford University Press.

Widstrands, C. C., (ed), 1970, *Cooperatives and Rural Development in East Africa,* New York: African Publishing Co.

5

Cooperatives During Independence and The Rise of Socialism

This chapter analyzes the cooperative sector during independence and the rise of socialism. We explore the rapid expansion of the cooperative movement and the problems encountered. We also examine the rise and implementation of socialist policy and the elusive role of cooperatives in villages and Ujamaa Villages.

5.1 Expansion of the Cooperative Movement

After Tanganyika (Tanzania Mainland) became independent in 1961, the government decided to embark on a systematic crash program for organizing cooperatives in areas of the Tanzanian mainland which, until then, were untouched by the movement. They targeted the central and coastal regions, Mtwara and Ruvuma in the south, and the west, even in areas where no cash crops nor surplus food crops were produced for sale. The government thought that cooperatives could help in achieving economic independence by having Africans control the economy through their cooperatives (The United Republic of Tanzania. 1966: 5; Hyden, 1976: 11).

With the expansion of the cooperative movement, the government established the Cooperative Union of Tanganyika Ltd. (CUT) which was registered on 27 November, 1961 as a national cooperative organization. Membership to CUT. was open to all cooperative unions in the country and such primary societies or other cooperative societies as were not affiliated to any other cooperative union. The general aim of the CUT. was to encourage the growth of the cooperative movement and promote the well-being of its members in accordance with cooperative principles and practices through the collection and dissemination of cooperative information.

The Cooperative Union of Tanganyika Ltd. (CUT), as an apex organization, had the following responsibilities:

a) To promote various types of cooperatives by educating the affiliated members on all matters pertaining to the cooperative movement as well as carrying out publicity work on behalf of the affiliated cooperative unions and societies;

b) To arrange the audit and supervision of affiliated societies and unions as may be authorized by the Registrar; and

c) To promote the well-being of cooperative unions according to cooperative principles. This was done through carefully examining all legislation affecting the movement with a view to influence it for the benefit of the cooperative members, and by providing them assistance in legal matters (CUT, 1961: 2).

During the 1960s the government had the intention to promote cooperatives in many parts of the country because the government saw cooperatives as tools for economic development for the mass of small peasants. Importance was given to cooperative development to the extent that after independence one of the first ministries formed was the Ministry of Cooperatives and Community Development. The intention of the government to promote cooperatives in the farming sector was expressed in the Five Year Plan for Economic and Social Development 1964 -1969.

To facilitate a rapid expansion of the cooperative movement, the government changed the Cooperative Societies Ordinance in 1963 to give power to the minister responsible for cooperatives to permit registration of a cooperative society if he found it desirable, even if registration of such a society had been refused by the Registrar of Cooperatives because he was not satisfied as to the cooperative's viability (Tanganyika, Government (1963) Section 67). The registrar's decisions were subject to reversal by the minister on political, rather than economic grounds.

With government initiative, cooperatives were started in Dodoma, Singida, Mtwara, Coast, Morogoro and Kigoma regions[4]. The number of registered societies increased from 857 in 1961 to 1,533 in April 1966 (Cooperative Development Division, 1966: 41). Many of these cooperatives were started with very weak economic foundations as noted later:

> *The political pressures (after 1961) were considerable. Societies were organized from 'on top', without genuine local demand or even understanding, but in their enthusiasm in the first flush of freedom, people went along (The United Republic of Tanzania 1966(a): 5).*

It is argued that this rapid expansion due to government intervention led to inadequate preparation and members being uninformed as to the nature of their cooperatives (Minde, 1982: 43). Moreover, with this rapid cooperative expansion, there was a startling growth in the movement's demands for skilled manpower, and an equally great dilution in the government's skilled supervisory personnel (The United Republic of Tanzania 1966(a): 6).

The government gave cooperatives the monopoly to buy certain cash crops from peasants. The Agricultural Products (Control and Marketing) Act 1962 gave the Minister of Agriculture power to establish

---

4 The political decision to establish cooperatives without consideration of their economic viability caused many problems in the cooperative movement.

marketing boards which would have exclusive rights to market certain crops and rights to appoint agents. The National Agricultural Products Board (NAPB) was established under this Act in 1962. NAPB. handled maize, cashew nuts, paddy, groundnuts, sunflower seeds, simsim, copra, cassava, and other crops. The NAPB. appointed agricultural marketing cooperatives to buy crops from growers. Other big marketing boards were the Lint and Seed Marketing Board (LSMB) established in 1962, and the Tanganyika Coffee Board (TCB) established in 1962. These marketing boards bought crops from cooperative unions. By 1970, there were 12 marketing boards in Tanzania.

At independence, the cooperative movement was very popular with the political leadership of the country. The minister for agriculture, the late P. Bomani, who had been the General Manager of the Victoria Federation of Cooperative Unions (VFCU) from 1955 to 1960 wrote:

> *The coming independence and the birth of a nation was thought to be a most appropriate time to record the history of the cooperative movement in Tanganyika. On this happy occasion, I would like to acknowledge the part played by the co-operative movement in the struggle for the liberation of our country, a part which will go down in the annals of Tanganyikan history. In the moulding of our people into a nation, the co-operative movement has, had, and will continue to have an important role to play.*[5]

The cooperative societies were responsible for educating their members in the cooperative principles and practices. During the early years of independence in the 1960s, it took time to educate a farmer as to the rights and responsibilities of a member of a cooperative when the farmer's general education had been neglected. It took time to instruct a member of the cooperative committee (the governing body of every cooperative) as to their obligations to the members. It also took time to train a society secretary, rarely with more than a Standard VIII education and often with as little as a Standard IV education, in the handling of the book-keeping, the weighing and record keeping. As cooperative societies increased, production increased too, as reports showed:

> *The past five years (after 1961) have seen a great expansion in the cooperative movement. The volume of produce handled increased from 145,000 tons in 1961 to 496,000 tonnes in 1965.*[6] *Provision of education to members and staff in cooperatives was necessary for this expansion.*

5 Forward by Hon. P. Bomani in The Tanganyika government, 1962: 1

6 The United Republic of Tanzania (URT) 1966(a): 5

The main function of marketing boards was in the marketing of the crops collected from the primary societies. For instance, the Lint and Seed Marketing Board transported cotton from the warehouses of societies to the ginneries, supervised the ginning, controlled the lint cotton and cotton seed as soon as they were produced and it also operated a price assistance fund. At the extreme, the board licensed exporters and produced seeds to be exported. The marketing boards were responsible for arranging the final sale of crops after primary processing. The cotton lint was sold at public auctions.

5.1.1 The Cooperatives provided services to their Members and Public

Some cooperative unions like the KNCU, BNCU, and RACU had agricultural experiment stations. Cooperatives advised peasants to produce a high quality crop and in large quantities in order to earn a larger income from crop sales. They instructed peasants on the practices of good husbandry. They were ideal instruments through which to channel agricultural advice and credit programs (Saul, 1975: 206; Collinson, 1975: 259). Farm inputs could, in some cases, be purchased on credit through marketing cooperatives. Some marketing cooperatives provided peasants with good seeds to ensure good crops.

Marketing cooperatives played a role in training members to work in their communities. It was through membership in cooperatives that peasants developed the idea of democratic participation in decision-making in formal organizations. Members participated in meetings, voted over issues, and elected committee members and a chairman (Ngeze, 1975: 46). Cooperatives helped to train. Some early nationalist leaders emerged from the cooperative movement. For instance, after independence, these cooperative leaders: Paul Boman (VFCU), George Kahama (BNCU), Nsilo Swai (Meru-Arusha Cooperative Union) and Jeremeah Kasambala (RACU), among the ministers of the first cabinet of Tanganyika.[7] These people were trained for leadership in the cooperative movement and later provided leadership in the government.

Marketing cooperatives educated cooperators and the general public. Efforts were made to train the cooperative staff. In the 1950's, secretaries of primary societies were trained at Mzumbe Cooperative School while inspectors and staff of the cooperative unions were sent out of the country for training This changed when the Moshi Cooperative College was established in 1963 as it became the principal institution of cooperative training. This college provided courses for primary society secretaries, cooperative inspectors, cooperative managers, and other

7 The transfer of able officers from the cooperative movement to Party and government posts deprived the movement of some of its capable and qualified personnel.

staff in the cooperative movement. The Moshi Cooperative College and the Cooperative Education Centre had programs to educate the general public on cooperatives. Part of the education fund in the marketing cooperatives was used to provide general education. Marketing cooperatives also gave financial assistance to schools. For instance, the KNCU. built Lyamungo Secondary School in Kilimanjoro region.

5.1.2 *Problems in Cooperatives*

The cooperatives also faced many problems. The general situation in Tanzania was that most cooperative committee members were not only untrained when it came to their specific technical responsibilities, but that they also possessed a low standard of formal education. Thus, it became difficult for them to cope with the complex issues of development, which marketing cooperatives were supposed to tackle. Inefficient management was also a great obstacle that hindered the achievement of a high level of efficiency and effectiveness.

There was an inability to control losses which arose from an actual shrinkage of produce due to loss of moisture, pilferage, padded produce receipts, incorrect grading, and losses incurred while produce was in transit from societies to buying agents. The problem in most marketing cooperatives was that standardized equipment and methods for establishing correct measures were rarely used.

The government and the TANU ruling political parties intervened to control marketing cooperatives. Their intervention came in the form of policy guidelines, administrative measures, which were normally absorbed during the registration process, or government directives and policy statements.

The Department of Cooperative Development (DCD), a government organ, had ambitious plans to manage cooperatives. However, the department faced various problems such as inadequate personnel for supervisory, inspection and surveillance services, and for other technical services that cooperatives required. It had inadequate transport facilities for field officers to visit cooperatives in the villages. It was preyed upon by inefficient administration, not only because of overloaded tasks, but also because of its more rigid and bureaucratic approach to business problems, which instead required foresight and dynamism.

The President of Tanzania, Mwalimu Julius K. Nyerere, appointed a Special Committee of Enquiry into the Cooperative Movement and Marketing Boards on 26th January 1966 with the following terms of reference:

(design: block quote here to review staffing and where necessary, the organizational structure of the cooperative movement and marketing boards in order to recommend what steps should be taken to strengthen them for the maximum benefit of the producers and consumers alike.[8]

On 25th March 1966, the Department of Cooperative Development was asked by the Economic Committee of the Cabinet to cover the question of recruitment of new members by the cooperatives. This special committee submitted its report on 1st June 1966 and later the same year the government published a response to that report (URT, 1966(b)).

The Special Committee of Enquiry reported that the general structure of the agricultural cooperative movement was sound and that the defects were a result of its growth. The committee listed the following five basic defects:

a) Uninformed members - there were many societies whose members were uninformed about the nature of cooperatives, how they were supposed to function, and the duties of members assembled in the general meeting. Even less was understood about the relationship between the union and the various marketing boards, and between various levels of cooperatives and the government.

b) Shortage of appropriate manpower to staff the cooperatives - the common issue in the manpower situation was the fact that cooperative employees did not adequately regard themselves as a professional group that had qualities such as ethical standards, career possibilities, and opportunities for growth. Employees were regularly dishonest and often in adequately trained.

c) Lack of democracy at the union level - in many ways, farmers did not regard the union as belonging to them. Often, it was thought of as an arm of the government. The society representatives at the general meeting of the Union were often too uniformed to use their powers wisely.

d) Experience of members - there was a marked absence of groups of skilled people who could be called upon to render advice on problems beyond the scope of members and of the staff whose experience had been confined to the general management of agricultural cooperative matters. Cooperatives had no qualified staff to deal with transport problems, negotiations and drafting contracts

e) The susceptibility of the cooperative movement to political interference - political decisions, however sound in intent, were

8 The United Republic of Tanzania, 1966: 1

misinterpreted so as to justify exaggerated demands for the premature registration of societies, which was a root cause of those problems.[9]

After identifying the existing problems, the Commission of Enquiry made the following recommendations:

a) Formation of a Unified Cooperative Service (UCS) which would be a commission which would among other things, ensure employment of appropriate manpower to staff cooperatives. The UCS would be responsible for employing discipline, terms of service and dismissal of employees of cooperatives.

b) Training of both cooperative employees and ordinary members needed to be improved so as to develop skilled people who knew their responsibilities within the cooperative.

c) Registration of only the cooperatives that were deemed viable, at performance of their activities. This could be achieved through strengthening the cooperatives especially in their supervisory functions in relation to member societies with the long term aim of making them assume greater responsibility in all matters pertaining to the development of the cooperative movement.

d) The establishment of specialized service departments within the Cooperative Union of Tanzania. One of the departments would prepare and mount an intensive members' education and information campaign on cooperatives throughout the country. This could help the expansion of informed members to the cooperative movement all over the country.

e) The election of a union committee should be done directly by the members and an electoral commission be established at the Cooperative Union of Tanzania Ltd, to deal with the complaints. This would ensure democracy among the members of the cooperatives that would be associated with cooperative principles

f) To strengthen the power of the registrar and dissolve the Victoria Federation of Cooperative Union and the Tanganyika Cooperative Trading Agency. (The United Republic of Tanzania 1966: 13-40).

The government response to the report of the Presidential Special Committee of Enquiry was contained in Government Paper number 3 of 1966 (URT, 1966(b)). The government accepted the report and all the criticisms and recommendations except those that were associated with political interference and the election of union committee members. The government saw nothing basically undemocratic in the procedure

9 The United Republic of Tanzania(URT) 1966(a). pp. 10-11.

of electing union committee members among delegates from primary societies, who were themselves democratically elected.

Regarding political interference, the government felt that by their very nature, cooperatives could not be isolated from political life because it was government policy to employ the economic aim of cooperation to achieve the political aim of socialism. In this way, it was inevitable and also necessary that the two should mix from time to time. The government also accepted the idea of a unified cooperative service and of strengthening the CUT. Recommendations to strengthen the power of the registrar, the dissolution of the Victoria Federation, and the Tanganyika Cooperative Trading Agency were also accepted (URT, 1966(b)).

In the early years of independence (1961 to 1966), there were achievements which were fundamental for cooperative development. Such achievements included the establishment of the Cooperative Union of Tanganyika (CUT) in 1961, the enactment of the Cooperative Societies Act in 1963 The enactment of the Agricultural Products (Control and Marketing) Act in 1962 empowered the minister of agriculture to establish marketing boards. Also, the National Agricultural Products Board (NAPB) was formed in 1963 to deal with food crops, and the National Cooperative and Development Bank (NCDB), was established in 1964, and was intended to channel credit to smallholder farmers. The appointment of the Presidential Special Committee of Enquiry to the Cooperatives and Marketing Boards in January 1966 and its report in June 1966 were instrumental in solving the farmers' grievances and complaints (URT, 1966(a)).

The implementation of the recommendations of the Presidential Special Committee of Enquiry was as follows:

Dissolution of the Victoria Federation of Cooperative Union, which had faced serious problems of corruption and inefficiency resulting from the inability of members to exercise effective control at the primary society level. Due to this situation, the government proposed measures to intervene in affairs of the federation. In the resulting reorganization, the federation merged with its unions to form the Nyanza Cooperative Union in 1967. New management was appointed and all staff of the federation and the old Unions were either dismissed or re-employed on new terms.

The Presidential Special Committee of Enquiry also recommended the dissolution of the Tanganyika Cooperative Trading Agency because Tanganyika Coffee Board (TCB) which had more experience and better facilities than TACTA, was performing the same functions.

The Presidential Special Committee of Enquiry recommended the establishment of the Unified Cooperative Service Commission (UCSC), which would have ultimate power over all personnel employed in cooperatives over such issues as uprooting corruption, nepotism, and dishonesty through the recruitment of the right personnel and the establishment of rules and procedures to check on such malpractices. Thus, in 1968 the UCSC was established by an Act of Parliament to perform such activities as advising employing societies regarding training awards, coordination and arrangement for courses of training, making provisions necessary for the maintenance and control of the services and pension schemes.

The Presidential Special Committee of Enquiry fURThermore recommended increasing the statutory powers of the registrar of the cooperative societies. Under this recommendation, the registrar was given powers to suspend or remove a committee or members of staff of any cooperative as a measure to improve efficiency. The Cooperative Societies Act of 1968 gave the registrar of cooperatives these powers (URT, 1966(a)).

The government's intervention in the cooperative movement had significant impacts. Empowerment of the minister for agriculture by the government interfered with the powers of the registrar of cooperatives such that even in cases in which the registrar would not agree to register a cooperative, his decision could be overruled. Consequently, cooperatives were established on political basis even in places where they were not economically viable. Hence, cooperatives emerged in many parts of the country and encountered various problems.

Many peasants tended to regard the cooperatives which were started under government pressure as arms of the government. Unlike the older marketing cooperatives, the new cooperatives, which were started in the country by the government's crash program were not readily accepted by peasants. Members of the new cooperatives were not involved in democratic control of their cooperatives and government intentions in these cooperatives were not fully understood by the peasants, many of whom had joined chiefly for the social and economic services offered.

5.2 Rural Socialism and Cooperatives

The Arusha Declaration, which was promulgated in January 1967, called for building Ujamaa in Tanzania.[10] The cooperative movement was

10 Ujamaa Policy is explained in these basic documents: "The Arusha Declaration: "Socialism and Self Reliance." and "Socialism and Rural Development," Reprinted in Nyerere 1968: 231-250; 337-366 respectively.

reorganized to make it possible for cooperatives to participate more in socialist construction and national development.

5.2.1 *Diversifying Activities of the Marketing Cooperatives*

The government saw marketing cooperatives as potential instruments for rural development, because cooperatives touched the peasants directly. In emphasizing this point the government stated:

> *"There is no other type of organization which is so suited to the problem and concept of rural development... It would be impossible for the government's administrative machinery to deal with individuals requiring government assistance and services, including credit for raising production and productivity. Without the use of cooperatives, the number of people wanting government help will make dissemination of government services and assistance financially very expensive and administratively almost impossible" (Government of Tanzania Paper No. 4, 1967).*

Following a recommendation by the Presidential Special Committee of Enquiry into the Cooperative Movement and Marketing Boards in 1966, the government passed the Cooperative Societies Act, 1968 which repealed and replaced the Cooperative Societies Ordinance of 1963. The Cooperative Societies Act, 1968 gave the registrar of cooperatives a wide range of discretionary powers over cooperatives (URT, 1968).

From 1968 onwards, the government also decided to amalgamate cooperatives to create Regional Cooperative Unions. It seems that the initial reasons for amalgamating cooperatives were primarily economic or financial (Hyden, 1976: 15). In some cases, the desire to amalgamate cooperatives did not emanate from the cooperatives, but instead, was a government policy aimed at extending central control over rural development processes. The amalgamation of cooperatives was achieved with relative ease in those areas where cooperative unions were already weak financially or where the leadership had developed alliances with the central political leadership of the country. Thus, in the Mtwara, Tanga, Mbeya, Kigoma, Iringa and Arusha regions, agreements to amalgamate the smaller unions developed through a combination of central pressure and local consent. Despite this, some economically strong cooperatives unions like the KNCU. and the BNCU did not see the benefit of amalgamating with weaker unions. The KNCU. did not like having to amalgamate with the Vuasu Cooperative Union Ltd. For example, their management committees felt that amalgamation could lead to financial strains on their Unions (Hyden, 1976: 15). Despite such resistance, the government called for compulsory amalgamation (Cooperative Societies Act, 1968 Section 73), and by 1974 all regions had their regional cooperative unions.

Another important step to the transformation of cooperatives during the late 1960's was the increasing of the statutory powers of the Registrar of Cooperative Societies. According to the Cooperative Societies Act of 1968, the registrar was given power to suspend or remove members of staff of any cooperative as a measure to improve efficiency. Before the act, only the minister of cooperatives had such power.

The tendency of the Tanzania government to intervene in encouraging and supervising the cooperative movement seemed to exist for two reasons. Firstly, to encourage the establishment of cooperatives to defend people against exploitation and at the same time to achieve modernization. Secondly, government assistance was essential to the expansion of the movement to ensure that cooperatives provided services to their members (Nyerere, 1973(a): 131).

Under the Ujamaa policy, the agricultural marketing cooperatives were assigned a new role which was specified in the Arusha Declaration:

> *To build and maintain socialism it is essential that all the major means of production and exchange in the nation are controlled and owned by peasants through the machinery of their government and their cooperatives (Nyerere, 1968: 233-234).*

Recall the major function which agricultural cooperatives performed was that of selling farm products.[11] Because cooperative members desired to have democratic control of their business enterprise, cooperative marketing eliminated middlemen who exploited individual crop sellers. Cooperative primary societies bought crops from farmers on a non-profit basis and either sold them at the market or forwarded them to marketing boards for sale[12] (see Fig. 1). If the cooperative realized any surplus, it was distributed to its members on a patronage basis after all necessary deductions such as providing a contingency reserve, paying dividends on capital stock, and enriching the educational fund.

---

11 Marketing is related to the flow of goods and services from the point of initial production until they are received by consumers.

12 Cooperative unions were buying agents of marketing boards. It is argued that the nature of this agency relationship is that it was imposed from above rather than through a mutually beneficial arrangement. (Minde, 1982). That is, cooperative unions were required by marketing boards to sign agency contracts. Cooperatives bought crops from peasants and sold them to the boards at prices fixed by the government.

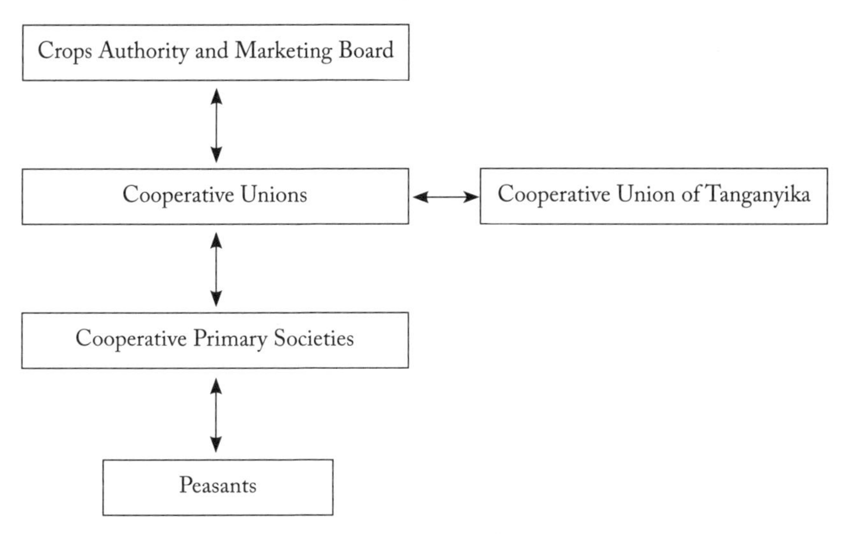

Fig. 1 Organizational Structure of Agricultural Marketing Up to 1976

Thus, cooperatives were instruments of economic development. In promoting agricultural development, cooperatives encouraged the production of certain strategic crops by providing farm inputs and processing and selling their products (Hedlund, 1998: 71).

The Arusha Declaration of 1967 contained socialist and self-reliance policies. Socialism, according to Julius Nyerere (Nyerere, 1968), President of Tanzania, is an attitude which includes a deeply felt sense of obligation for the welfare of the people. Its objectives were self-reliance, rural development, equity, and national economy control (Forster, P.G and Maghimbi, S. (editors) 1992: 63).

The Arusha Declaration introduced Ujamaa policy in Tanzania and production in rural areas was to be realized either by the state or through cooperatives. Marketing cooperatives were seen as key instrument for building socialism and realizing rural development. The cooperative movement therefore was to be re-organized.

5.2 Villages and Ujamaa Villages

The Ujamaa Policy recommended the establishment of Ujamaa villages. These ideal, Ujamaa villages were economic and social communities where people were to live together for the good of all (Nyerere, 1968: 348). An Ujamaa village was a cooperative agricultural production unit that would foster both socialist principles and rural transformation. An Ujamaa village emphasized equality, cooperation and democracy. The village members were expected to own and control the means of production collectively and in a democratic manner (Nyerere, 1968: 352).

President Nyerere emphasized that moves toward Ujamaa had to be made voluntarily by members through their own efforts. The use of force to promote Ujamaa was rejected. President Nyerere wrote:

> *Ujamaa villages are intended to be socialist organizations created by the people and governed by those who live and work in them. --- An Ujamaa village is a voluntary association of people who decide of their own free will to live together and work together for their common good (Nyerere, 1973 (a): 67).*

The principle of voluntary implementation in the building of Ujamaa villages followed Nyerere's analysis of the Tanzanian rural social formations and their ideologies which, despite a certain process of economic differentiation going on, he found to include traditional communalism and egalitarian attitudes favorable to Ujamaa development.

Nyerere was aware of economic differentiation in the country, but he judged it to be too weak to have an impact on the implementation of the Ujamaa policy.

He wrote:

> *The small-scale capitalist agriculture we now have is not really a danger; but our feet are on the wrong path, and if we continue to encourage or even help the development of agricultural capitalism, we shall never become a socialist state. On the contrary, we shall be continuing the break up of the traditional concepts of human equality based on sharing all the necessities of life and on a universal obligation to work (Nyerere, 1968: 344).*

Ujamaa in the rural areas was intended to combat growing rural class formation through the encouragement of village producer cooperatives. A number of different processes of differentiation and class formation could be distinguished in rural areas, each related in one way or another to the development of commodity production.

The earliest development of African commodity production during the colonial period occurred on the more fertile highland areas such as in Kilimanjaro, Bukoba, and Rungwe, where coffee was cultivated. These areas had a relatively high population density, which stimulated an intensified system of production. But high-density population coupled with the limitation on the transfer of land limited the opportunities for accumulation through increased land holding and diverted surplus produce into other channels such as investment in education, trade, or business.

The commercial production of tobacco, cotton, and cereals such as wheat, maize and paddy by Africans enabled them to accumulate wealth, which they invested in commodity production, petty trade, and business ventures. These progressive farmers of tobacco, cotton, and cereals emerged in the maize zone of Iringa, the wheat zone of Mbulu and Hanang', the tobacco area of Tabora, and the cotton zone of South West Lake Victoria in the 1950's and 1960's, when the government agricultural policy encouraged progressive farmers by offering them extension services and agricultural credit. The rich farmers employed casual labour for cultivating, planting, weeding, and harvesting periods.

International capital has its requirements for the export of crops and for the production process, which allows the maximum degree of control through technical subordination; that is, by processes which are dependent upon mechanical, chemical, and biological inputs whose technology is ultimately controlled by international capital. Sales of Tanzania's agricultural products at international markets are faced with the depressing menace of low prices and income elasticities of demand, rapid growth of synthetic substitutes, tariffs, various protection policies in the agricultural sector of the developed world, and shipping cartels extracting high freight charges.

The state extracts surplus through its control by means of which it sets the terms of exchange facing the peasant producers. The reproduction and development of a rich peasantry depends on the development of property and the legal relations of generalized commodity production. Under Ujamaa, the chances of developing a rich peasantry were slim. The Ujamaa policy legalized action against factors that would increase socio-economic differentiation in Ujamaa villages. The setting of legal maximum farm sizes, price control, taxation systems, and the inadequate importation of agricultural machinery, spare parts and certain goods all worked against the growth of the capitalist farmers and forecast their demise.

After the adoption of the Ujamaa policy, peasants began to organize themselves into Ujamaa villages. In some cases peasants themselves made the decision to establish villages as attempts at self-reliant cooperative development. In other cases peasants were induced through ideological persuasion and material incentives to move into villages and start communal farming. In such cases the government and the TANU. leaders persuaded peasants to move from scattered homestead areas and come together to form villages so that services such as water supply, schools and health centers could be easily provided.

Maghimbi listed some objectives of Ujamaa villages (Forster and Maghimbi (eds) (1992):

a) To improve the technology of rural life so as to increase efficiency in producing social and economic services as well as the extension of services, credit, input supply, marketing facilities, and storage;

b) To combine individual plots into a large single farm on which modern farming practices could be applied;

c) To offer an opportunity for peasants to participate in social activities for the development of the country;

d) To enhance the revolution in crafts, farming, carpentry, weaving, and trade;

e) To improve the social and economic infrastructure and provide basic social services such as education, health, and water supply; and

f) To improve the marketing and distribution system of goods and services and promote rural development.

In establishing villages, there were some cases with an urgent need to bring people together into villages. Such areas as Dodoma in the year 1971, Chunya in 972, Kigoma in 1972, required moving people in large numbers at the same time into villages. The Party and government encouraged and helped peasants to leave areas such as those which were too dry and infertile or which had other ecological problems, and to move to better places.

To speed up the villagization program, TANU. resolved in 1973 that the whole rural population must live in villages by the end of 1976 (TANU, (1973): Resolution No.14 and 15). Villagization now became compulsory. The villagization program was effectively carried out, and it was reported in February, 1977 that the villagization program had been completed and that there were 13,065,000 people living together in 7,684 villages (Nyerere, 1977: 41). The progress of the villagization program 1970 – 1976 showed that the regional breakdown showed an uneven degree of villagization, with the heaviest concentration of new villages in the drier, less prosperous, and lower-density regions. Ellman (1974: 12) reported that 70% of the new established villages were in the five administrative regions with the lowest per capita Gross Domestic Product, while less than 10% were in the six administrative regions with highest per capital Gross Domestic Product. These poorer areas probably needed to be looked after first in terms of trying to lay a foundation for rapid socio-economic development.

Some peasants had reservations about moving away from land they had occupied for years. Other peasants resented the timing. The rich peasants saw clearly that Ujamaa villagization was working against their personal interests so they resented moving into Ujamaa villages. But with compulsory villagization, they had no choice but to be moved by force into villages. In some parts of the country compulsory villagization was not carried out smoothly. In some cases, bad village sites had been selected. The planning process did not consider all the factors necessary such as the land required for family settlement its water prospects, and other factors. In some areas, regional and district leadership looked into the availability of infrastructure and services and these were used as important factors regardless of the consequences for agriculture (Coulson, 1975: 53-58).

With compulsory villagization, there were widely publicized cases of misadministration and mistreatment of the people. Some leaders acted without any consultation with the people who were being moved. This left a legacy of bitterness which increased peasant suspicion of the bureaucracy. President Nyerere, in pointing out the problem of leadership in implementing villagization program, wrote:

> *...we had cases of people being required to move from an area of permanent water to an area which is permanently dry. We had other cases where the new villages were made too large for the land available. And there were cases where people were rounded up without notice, and dumped on the village site, without time to prepare shelter for themselves. These were examples of bad leadership and they made people very angry (Nyerere, 1977: 42).*

But we cannot generalize that these cases were typical of the whole villagization program. In some cases, people moved by their own volition and with assistance from TANU. and the government.

5.2.1 *Villages and Ujamaa Villages Functioning as Multi-Purpose Cooperative Societies*

In an effort to increase the involvement of cooperatives to implement the Ujamaa policy, the government directed that marketing cooperatives had to do more than market crops. Cooperatives were required to carry on the production of farm crops (The United Republic of Tanzania, 1969: 31-32).

Due to an amendment that was made in the Cooperatives Societies Act, 1968, the government directed in October 1971, that villages which had reached a high stage of development could be registered under the Cooperative Societies Act, 1968 as multi-purpose cooperative societies for producing, processing, and marketing farm products (The Tanzania Standard Newspaper, 22 October, 1971).

The second Five Year Development Plan (1969-1974) required the cooperative movement to be changed to assume a new structure which would be based on cooperative farming units at the primary level, and which would allow increased democratic participation by members in the control of all cooperative activities. The development plan required the marketing cooperatives to involve the farmers in cooperative production instead of concentration on the collection and marketing of farm products. (The United Republic of Tanzania, 1969).

The new structure of cooperatives was achieved through the formation of village multipurpose cooperatives, or Ujamaa villages, and orienting marketing-based societies towards additional activities more directly affecting production. But the formation of village cooperatives contributed to the fURTher collapse of marketing cooperatives. This was due to a decision made by TANU that all Tanzanians in rural areas should live in the villages by the end of 1976. The villagization process went hand-in-hand with the transformation of marketing cooperatives into village cooperatives. Production and marketing activities were to be done by village cooperatives. In 1971 the government decided to register villages as multi-purpose cooperative societies which would perform crop production and crop marketing activities.

Marketing cooperatives were given the task of forming village cooperatives. This hindered marketing cooperatives from undertaking their own business and kept them occupied implementing government and party policies for forming village cooperatives. In doing this, the marketing cooperatives underwent a self-elimination process as they were automatically transferring their roles to the village cooperatives.

Villages that registered as cooperative societies were able to get credit from financial institutions, especially from the Tanzania Rural Development Bank and the National Bank of Commerce. By selling crops through village cooperatives, more villagers were expected to have control of the marketing institution. By the end of 1973, there were 380 Ujamaa villages registered as Multi-purpose Cooperative Societies.

The registration of village cooperatives under the Cooperative Societies Act, 1968, was later considered to not be in line with the national policy of Ujamaa Villages, and it was not leading to the envisaged rural transformation. Villages which were registered under the Cooperative Societies Act, 1968 were recognized as cooperatives and not as villages any longer. This was contrary to the national rural policy of building Ujamaa villages. For this reason, TANU. directed the government to pass a bill to recognize and register Villages and Ujamaa villages. This was also an extension of the 1972 decentralization program to empower people at the village level (Nyerere, 1973 (b)). This also was in line with the TANU. Guidelines 1971 which directed that people should participate in deciding and implementing their socio-economic affairs (Tanganyika African National Union, 1971 Section 28).

Conclusion

TANU felt that the cooperative unions had developed into complex structures that failed to enable members at grassroots levels to follow the progress of others and to exercise effective control. It was reported in the media that there was widespread corruption and misappropriation of cooperatives' funds by employees and committee members. The media publically criticized the affairs of cooperatives. These criticisms eroded not only the morale and commitment of members towards their cooperative movement, but also negatively influenced policy-makers and the general public. This became a factor which contributed significantly towards the withdrawal of government support for the movement.

During the period 1967-1976, marketing cooperatives were in great crisis due to deliberate government plans to implement its commitments to the policy of socialism and self-reliance. The government feared the powers of marketing cooperatives and their influence over the social, economic, and cultural activities of the population.

Thus, the Tanzanian government intervention in the cooperative movement resulted in cooperatives being formed on a top-down basis without sufficient consideration of their economic viability, the availability of trained manpower, or in most instances, the desires of the members themselves.

References

Cliffe, L. and J.S. Saul (eds.), 1973, Socialism in Tanzania in *An Interdisciplinary Reader* Vol.2, Dar es Salaam: East African Publishing House.

Cliffe, L. Peter Lawrence,William Luttre, Shem Migot-Adhola and John S. Saul (eds.), 1975, *Rural Cooperation in Tanzania,* Dar es Salaam: Tanzania Publishing House.

Collinson, M., 1975, 'Tanzania Cooperative Movement and Farmer Credit in 1960s' in Cliffee, L., L.P. Lawrence, W. Luttrel, Shem-Migot-Adhola and John S. Saul (eds.), 1975, *Rural Cooperation in Tanzania,* Dar es Salaam: Tanzania Publishing House.

Cooperative Development Division, 1966, *Notes on Cooperative Movement in Tanzania,* Dar es Salaam: Government Printer.

Cooperative Union of Tanganyika (CUT), 1961, *By-Laws of the Cooperative Union of Tanganyika Ltd.,* Dar es Salaam: Government Printer.

Coulson, A., 1975, 'Peasants and Bureaucrats' *in Review of African Political Economy,* 3: 53-58.

Ellman, A.O., 1974, 'Progress, Problems and Prospects in Ujamaa Development in Tanzania', ERB Paper 70: 18, Dar es Salaam: University of Dar es Salaam, Unpublished.

Forster, P. G and Maghimbi, S., 1992, *The Tanzanian Peasantry Economy in Crisis,* Aldershot: Ashgate Publishing Company.

Hedlund, H., 1998, *Cooperatives,* Uppsala: Scandinavian Institute of African Studies.

Hyden, G., 1976, *Cooperatives in Tanzania. Problems of Organization Building.* Dar es Salaam: Tanzania Publishing House.

Hyden, G., 1980, *Beyond Ujamaa in Tanzania: Underdevelopment and an Uncaptured Peasantry,* Berkley and Los Angeles: University of California Press.

Hyden, G., 1983, *Efficiency versus Distribution in East African Cooperatives: A study of Organizational Conflicts,* Uppsala: East African Studies.

Kjekshus H., 1977, 'The Tanzania villagization Policy: Implementation Lessons and Ecological Dimensions', in *Canadian Journal of African Studies,* XI, 2: 269-282.

Lyimo, F.F., 1983, Peasant Production and Cooperative Experiences in Tanzania: Case study of villages in Moshi and Urambo Districts. Ph.D Dissertation submitted to the University of Wisconsin-Madison.

McHenry, D.E., 1978, 'Peasant Participation in Communal Farming. The Tanzanian Experience, *in The African Studies Review,* 20, 3: 43-63.

Minde, E.M., 1982, The Changing Nature of Cooperatives and the Law, L.L.M. dissertation. University of Dar es Salaam.

Mwansasu, B.U and C. Pratt, 1979, *Toward Socialism in Tanzania,* Toronto: University of Toronto Press.

Ngeze, P., 1975, *Ushirika Tanzania,* Dar es Salaam: Tanzania Publishing House.

Nyerere J.K., 1973, (b), *Decentralization,* Dar es Salaam: National Printing Company Ltd.

Nyerere, J.K., 1968, *Freedom and socialism* Dar es Salaam: Oxford University Press.

Nyerere, J.K., 1973, (a), *Freedom and Development,* Dar es Salaam: Oxford University Press.

Nyerere, J.K., 1977, *The Arusha Declaration Ten Years After,* Dar es Salaam: Government Printer.

Omari, C.K., 1976, *The Strategy for Rural Development: The Tanzanian Experience.* Dar es Salaam: East Africa Literature Bureau.

Saul, J.S., 'The Role of the Cooperative Movement' in Cliffe, L., Peter Lawrence, William Luttrel, Shem Migot-Adhola and J.S. Saul (eds.), 1975, *Rural Cooperation in Tanzania,* Dar es Salaam: Tanzania Publishing House,.

Tanganyika African National Union (TANU), 1971, *Mwongozo wa TANU,* Dar es Salaam: Government Printer.

Tanganyika African National Union (TANU), 1973, *Maazimio ya Mkutano Mkuu wa TANU wa 15 na 16,* Dar es Salaam: National Printing Company Ltd.

Tanganyika Government (1963) *Cooperative Societies Ordinance,* Dar es Salaam: The Government Printer.

The Tanganyika Government, 1962, *The Cooperative Movement in Tanganyika,* Dar es Salaam: Tanganyika Standard Ltd.

The United Republic of Tanzania (URT), 1966a, *Report of The Presidential Special Committee of Enquiry into Co-operative Movement and Marketing Boards,* Dar es Salaam: Government Printer.

The United Republic of Tanzania (URT), 1968, *Cooperative Societies Act, 1968,* Dar es Salaam: Government Printer.

The United Republic of Tanzania (URT) (1969) Plan for Economic and social Development. July 1, 1969 – June 30, 1974. Vol.1 General analysis. Government Printer, Dar es Salaam.

United Republic of Tanzania (URT), 1966b, Proposals of Tanzania Government on the Recommendations of the Special Presidential Committee of Enquiry into the Cooperative Movement and Marketing Boards, Dar es Salaam: Government Printer, Government Paper No. 3-1966.

Widstrand, C.C., (ed.), 1970, *Cooperative and Rural Development in East Africa,* New York: African Publishing Company.

6

The Abolition of The Farmers' Marketing Cooperatives

This chapter analyzes the decline and eventual abolition of farmers' marketing cooperatives which were registered using the Cooperative Societies Act, 1968. The villages and Ujamaa villages as the basic units of cooperation are analyzed, followed by a discussion of the problems which marketing cooperatives faced, and of the government decision to abolish the marketing cooperative unions and their affiliated primary cooperative societies, which were operating in the villages registered under the Villages and Ujamaa Villages Act, 1975.

6.1 Villages as Basic Units of Cooperation

The government enacted the Villages and Ujamaa Villages Act, 1975 in order to speed up the socialist transformation process in rural areas and register the villages and Ujamaa villages under the Villages Act, 1975. Registered villages were recognized by the Villages Act, 1975, to function as multi-purpose primary cooperative societies. A village was an administrative and political entity with its own government.

The Villages and Ujamaa villages Act, 1975 recognized villages at two stages. In the first stage, a village was registered under the Act. Village registration was carried out when the registrar of villages was satisfied that not less than 250 households or family units had settled there and made their homes within an area of Tanganyika and that the boundaries of such an area could be defined (Villages and Ujamaa Villages Act, 1975 Section 4). Under this Act:

> *A village and its various organs shall perform their functions as if the village were a multi-purpose cooperative society; provided that the provisions of the cooperative societies act 1968 or of any subsidiary legislation there under shall not apply to a village or to any organ thereof (Villages and Ujamaa Villages Act, 1975 section 13).*

The Villages Act stated members of Village Assembly as follows: "Every person who was a resident in the village and had attained the age of 18 years was considered a member of the Village Assembly" (Villages and Ujamaa Villages Act 1975 Section 5 Sub-section 2).

The Act stated that its objectives and reasons were for the registration, designation and administration of villages and Ujamaa villages. In spite of this declaration, this Act directed villages and their various organs to perform their functions as if the villages were multi-purpose cooperative societies. However, there were no rules or guiding principles in the Villages Act of 1975 as to how villages were to function as cooperatives (United Republic of Tanzania 1981). There was no cooperative setting outside the village government. The termination of the application of the Cooperative Societies Act, 1968 on villages, and the passing of the Villages and Ujamaa Villages Act, 1975 with no cooperative details in the Act posed a problem of different interpretation of how villages were to function as cooperatives.

The Prime Minister's report on the Villages and Ujamaa Village Act, 1975 gave details of the cooperative content in the villages (Ofisi ya Waziri Mkuu na Makamu wa Pili wa Rais, 1975). The Prime Minister's report said that, in the first stage when a village was registered, a peasant could have his or her farm, but that farm machinery would belong to the village cooperative. Likewise, other village requirements like seeds, fertilizers, and expertise would be obtained through the village cooperative. In the second stage, a village was designated as an Ujamaa village. This could happen,

> *Where in relation to any village the Regional Party committee was satisfied that a substantial portion of economic activities of the village were being undertaken and carried out on a communal basis, the Regional committee would recommend to the Minister to designate the village as an Ujamaa village (Villages and Ujamaa villages Act, 1975 Section 16).*

The Act, 1975 did not define what it meant by the term 'substantial portion,' and left it to the discretion of Regional Party Committees (of the TANU. Party). Villages registered under the Villages and Ujamaa villages Act, 1975 were deemed to function as multi-purpose cooperative societies. Cooperative Societies which were registered under the Cooperative Societies Act, 1968 were not allowed to operate in a registered village. This resulted in decline of cooperative practice in villages.

6.2 Abolition of Farmers' Marketing Cooperatives

As a result of the restructuring of cooperatives in accordance with the Villages and Ujamaa villages Act, 1975 the TANU Party directed the government that the structure of the whole cooperative movement had to change to accommodate the changes that had taken place. On 14 May, 1976 the government of Tanzania abolished cooperative unions and their affiliated primary cooperative societies by the order of the Prime Minister, Rashid Kawawa. The few cooperatives based in urban areas such as retail shops, crafts, and industrial cooperatives, were not abolished. The government only abolished cooperative unions and their affiliated marketing primary cooperative societies in villages and Ujamaa Villages (Lyimo, 1983; Muungano wa vyama vya ushirika, 1977: 89).

The government abolished cooperative unions arguing that they mismanaged and misused members' resources. The government also claimed that cooperatives were capitalist institutions while the policy was to create socialist institutions and thus they warranted abolishment. Mwalimu Nyerere wrote that the cooperatives could not cope with the designated "Quick-March" to socialism and thus could not cater to government interests in fulfilling political and ideological aspirations as after all they were capitalist organizations (Banturaki J.A., 2000: 22). The view that marketing cooperatives were like middlemen was an idea expressed also by the Minister of Agriculture and Cooperatives in early 1970s.[13]

Marketing cooperatives in Tanzania which were abolished in 1976 suffered from both internal and external problems (Kimario 1992: 71-79).

Internal problems included the following:

a) Cooperatives were not supported by their members. Members of the cooperatives were not aware of their responsibilities and they believed that the cooperatives were not working for their interests;
b) The committee members were untrained, inexperienced, and unable to tackle the complex issues of the development of cooperatives;
c) There was a lack of management skills that caused problems in the recruitment of personnel and the supervision of day-to-day work in cooperatives; and
d) Cooperative members had very little or no knowledge on how to control their cooperatives and their services to member-users.

External problems were experienced through government and ruling party involvement in cooperatives (Kimario, 1992: 23):

a) Shortage of personnel in the Cooperative Development Division created a heavy burden on the field officers who in some instances failed to distinguish their priorities between going out to inspect cooperatives or remain in office to perform other duties;
b) Inadequate transportation to visit cooperatives in the villages hindered the deployment of field officers;
c) The Cooperative Development Department (C.D.D) was not effective enough because it was too rigid and bureaucratic in its approach to cooperative business. It had a centralized decision making process, rigid procedures of administration, a lack of proper coordination of the decisions made at different levels, and

---

13 In 1971 the then Minister of Agriculture and Cooperatives, D.N.M. Bryceson said that cooperatives were like middle men exploiting peasants, and that in future cooperative unions would be dissolved ("Coops head for Change to serve the Masses" in the Sunday News of 31st October, 1971)

a poor communication system which made it ineffective in dealing with cooperative business; and

d) The Cooperative Union of Tanganyika (CUT) was an organ of the TANU Party which meant the ruling party had direct influence through CUT on policy matters and the direction of the cooperative movement. TANU and CUT drifted apart because of the socialist policy. Cooperative unions were seen contradicting the socialist policy with activities incompatible with Ujamaa implementation.

After the government abolished the marketing cooperative unions and their affiliated cooperative primary societies, the functions of regional cooperative unions were relocated to marketing, trading, and commercial parastatal organizations and crop authorities where villages marketed their crops directly (Muungo wa Vyama vya Ushirika, 1977: 89). The abolition of marketing cooperatives had a number of consequences. In rural areas, stagnation and decline in agricultural production occurred. By law, villages were supposed to be multipurpose village cooperatives but in reality, they were not cooperatives because they failed to perform the required functions of cooperatives. They failed to provide agricultural inputs, credits, incentives, and efficient marketing. This directly contributed to the decline of the rural economy (Forster, P.G and S. Maghimbi (eds.) 1992: 228). The Government established Crop Authorities to perform marketing functions formerly carried out by cooperative unions. The Crop Authorities did the following:

a) Set up buying posts in every district so that they could buy crops from villages and supervised the transportation of goods from villages to their warehouses;

b) Advanced money to villages enabling them to buy crops from formers and perform functions such as weighing, packing and storage etc.;

c) Trained members of village council in product grading and handling so that they could assist in handling crops at a nominal fee;

d) Made arrangements to ensure the proper distribution of gunny bags, strings, sewing needles, scales and cash boxes; and

e) The Crop Authorities also advised the government and village council on how to improve crop production. Crop Authorities advised the Government on the market trends of product supply and prices (Forster, P.G and S. Maghimbi (eds.) 1992: 225).

The Crop Authorities were responsible for all major cash crops namely cotton, coffee, tobacco, tea, sisal, pyrethrum, and cashew nuts.

They were given the sole right to purchase and export these major crops. Another parastatal was the National Milling Corporation (N.M.C) which dealt with the major grain crops, that is maize, rice and wheat. N.M.C was given the sole right to buy food grains in the country and to import grains from other countries. Other cooperative services such as the wholesale and retail trades were taken over by state owned Regional Trading Companies (RTC).

Sam Maghimbi (Forster, P.G and Sam Maghimbi (eds) 1992) argued that the operation of crop authorities and state-owned trading companies impacted the peasants' economy. Parastatal monopolies became large consumers of government subsidies because of their bureaucratic nature and long chains of leadership positions, many of which represented political interests. This contributed to an increasingly high inflation rate which discouraged many peasants from producing crops and other products for the market.

The crop authorities and other marketing parastatals failed to provide services they had taken over from cooperative unions such as the provision of farm inputs such as fertilizers and seeds, as well as the provision of credits and tractors to peasants. There was also a decline or stagnation of the production of agricultural food and cash crops as the government did not pay enough attention to the agricultural sector because subsidies were used to fund parastatals instead of agriculture. This had a negative effect on peasants' morale and their motivation to improve farm production declined.

6.3 Villages Sold Crops Through Marketing Parastatals

Village cooperatives sold their crops directly to Crop Authorities and other marketing parastatals that were government institutions which operated at national regional and district levels but in which the peasant had no control (see Fig. 2). There was no provision for peasants to have a forum in these marketing institutions. There was no cooperative organization at the district or regional level to serve them.

At the national level, there was a Union of Cooperative Societies (UCS) in which Villages and Ujamaa villages were members (Acts supplement No. 9 of 1979 Section 5). UCS was a mass organization formed under the provisions of Article No. 70, sub-articles 1, 2 and 3 of the constitution of Chama Cha Mapinduzi (CCM)[14].

---

14 Chama Cha Mapinduzi has been the ruling Party in Tanzania and was established in February, 1977 by uniting the Afro-Shiraz Party of Zanzibar and the Tanganyika African National Union (TANU) of Tanganyika.

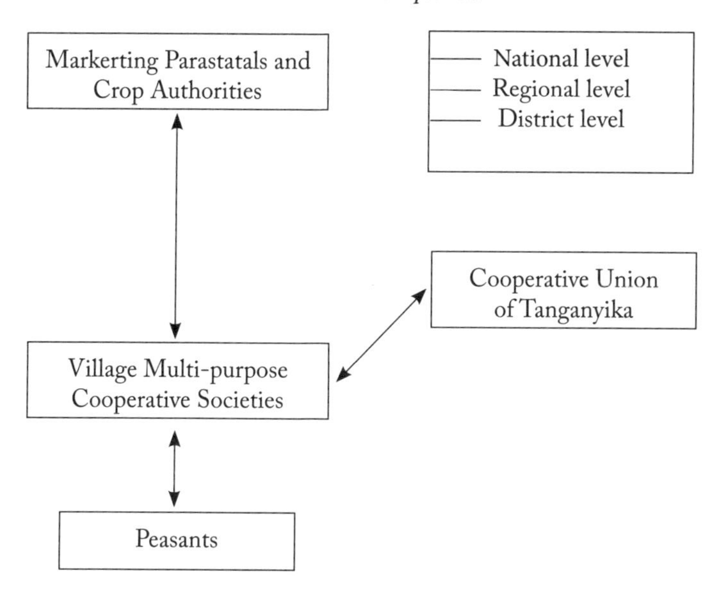

Fig. 2 Organizational Structure of Farm Products Marketing 1976 – 1981

The Union of cooperative societies was established in 1979 as a party organ with the aim of propagating the socialist ideology to rural and urban areas. It also acted as a pressure group for the ruling party in promoting other types of cooperatives in urban centers (Acts supplement No. 9 of 1979). The UCS did not have marketing functions of farm products and UCS had no link with the marketing parastatals.

Village multi-purpose cooperatives increased the number of cooperators in the villages. Being 18 years of age and also resident within a village were the two criteria for attaining cooperative membership in a village.

Each village council prepared articles of incorporation and by-laws which specified the policies, objectives, and goals of the village functioning as a multi-purpose cooperative. Members controlled their village activities when they participated in the decision making process, which occurred at annual Village Assembly meetings. All major decisions such as annual plans, budget, and election of village council were made and/or approved by the Village Assembly where members voted on issues presented. Members also participated indirectly in decision making by delegating power to the village council. Members could communicate their views to representatives in the village council and in various committees.

When a village was established, the Registrar issued the first village council with a certificate of incorporation. Upon the issue of such a certificate, the village council became a corporate body with perpetual succession and a common seal, and it was capable by law of suing and being sued in its corporate name.

The village members elected their village council members during village assembly election meeting. But if at the time of an election there was a CCM Party branch in the village, the Chairman and Secretary of the Party branch became by virtue of their Party leadership positions. Chairman and Secretary, respectively of the Council (Villages and Ujamaa Villages Act, 1975 Section 10(1)). By making the Party branch leaders to be leaders of a village council, Party control was brought into the administrative affairs of the village thus extending the concept of 'Party Supremacy' down to the village multi-purpose cooperative. This imposition of power could help to eliminate any potential conflict of interest between the Party branch leadership and the village council leadership. On the other hand, such imposition of power could be interpreted as denying the village assembly the opportunity to elect the Chairman and Secretary of the village government. As a matter of cooperative principle, this denial of village assembly democratic control over the top village council leadership was a serious matter where Party members were a minority in a village[15] because Party branch chairman is elected by Party members only. Also, should the village assembly be unsatisfied with such a chairman, it was not possible for the village assembly to remove the chairman from leadership because the Party constitution allowed a term of office of five years, and the removal of a village CCM party branch chairman or secretary from leadership would require sanction by the CCM party at the district or higher levels.

To plan and execute the daily cooperative activities in the villages, the village council appointed its committees among the village council members. The most common village committees were: Security and Defense committee, Production and Marketing committee, Planning and Financial committee, Construction and Transport committee and Education and Social welfare committee. The village council could appoint sub-committees in charge of specific projects such as shops, industries, and savings and credit (Fig. 3).

The supreme authority of the cooperative was in the village assembly where powers were vested in the village council. The village council, which consisted of delegates who were elected by the village assembly, was given powers to decide all activities necessary for the economic and social development of the village. The Village Act, 1975 recognized the village council as a corporate body with powers to own property, to enter into contracts, and to sue or to be sued. The village assembly was made up of all the villagers who had reached the age of 18 years. One of its major responsibilities was to elect representatives to the village council. The village assembly also received reports and made decisions on matters tabled in the village assembly meeting.

15 In a study, Minde (1982) found that Nkutabi village in Dodoma (Urban) district had 287 CCM Members against 1,112 villagers who qualified in age to be CCM members but were not members.

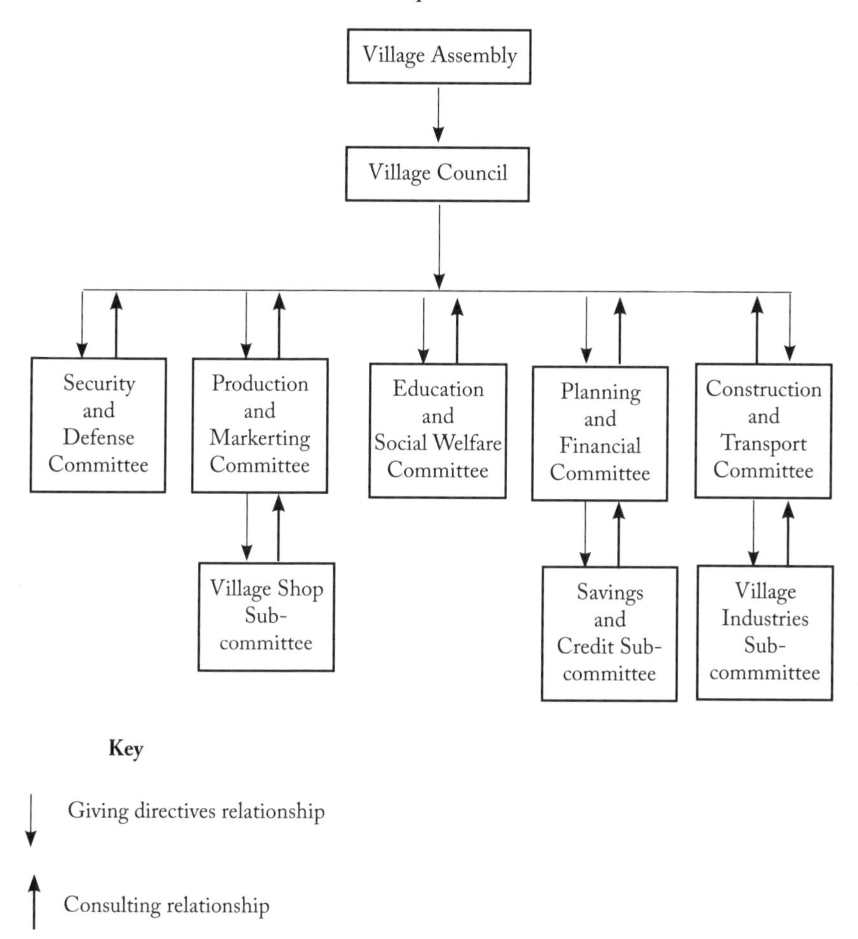

Fig. 3 Structural Relationship of Village Government

The structure of the cooperative movement consisted of village multi-purpose cooperatives and the Union of Cooperative Societies (UCS). Primary societies were the villages, Ujamaa villages, and various types of cooperatives in urban areas. The urban cooperatives were registered under the Cooperative Societies Act, 1968 and the villages and Ujamaa villages were registered and operated under the Village Act 1975. The urban cooperatives consisted of all types of cooperatives which were formed by workers and urban dwellers. The most common urban cooperative societies were consumer, housing, savings and credit, and industrial.

According to the Villages Act, 1975, the villages and Ujamaa villages were recognized as multipurpose production-oriented cooperatives and in principle this meant that economic life in the villages was conducted cooperatively. The villages exhibited the following major differences from marketing cooperatives:

First, residents of a village who had reached the age of 18 years were automatically accepted as members of the registered village. The idea here was to make all farmers in a village members of the village cooperative, regardless of whether they were willing to belong or not. This kind of compulsory membership was against the spirit of cooperative practice and against the principle of open membership;

Second, democratic machinery of the villages was such that the village assembly did not have much say about who was to be either chairman or secretary because these officials were imposed from above by the ruling party by virtue of being the village Party leaders. This was also not in conformity with the democratic principle of electing leaders which cooperatives believe to be the cornerstone of any organization which has identified itself as a cooperative society (ICA, 1975);

Third, formation and registration of villages was guided by political and administrative considerations rather than the economic viability and interests of members. In this spirit, cooperative members were not involved in decisions on the registration of the villages and in determining ways and means of conducting business in the best interest of their village cooperatives; and

Fourth, villages and Ujamaa villages operated as appendages of the Crop Authorities and marketing parastatals when it came to handling the villages' produce. This factor made it impossible for villages to influence the marketing forces in their favor and drastically reduced their autonomy as business organizations.

The Union of cooperative Society (UCS) was given the responsibility to see to it that party policies were implemented in accordance with the ruling party constitution. The UCS was expected to attune the attitude and economic lifestyle of cooperative members to the socialist ideals stipulated in the Arusha Declaration. The representative role of the UCS within the CCM party was only as a pressure group. In day-to-day activities, the UCS and the primary cooperative societies were guided by decisions made in the following forums:

a) The district forum was the lowest decision making organ of the UCS and it was composed of representatives from all cooperative organizations in the district, party officials (party chairmen and secretaries), members of parliament within the district, and government officers (district cooperative officer, district agricultural officer). The role of the district forum was to elect a district chairman and to elect ten committee members and representatives to the regional forum. The chairman and committee members were responsible for matters appertaining to the day-to-day operation of the UCS at the district office and policy matters concerning all types of cooperatives in the district (Act Supplement No. 9 of 1979);

b) The regional forum consisted of representatives from the district forum as well as the government and the party. The role of the forum was the same as the district forum with the only exception being that it concerned itself with policies at the regional level. The forum elected a chairman and committee members and representatives to the national forum (Act Supplement No.9 of 1979); and

c) The national forum consisted of representatives from all regions of the Tanzanian mainland, 15 representatives from Zanzibar, and representatives from the ruling party. It was the highest cooperative policy making body in the country. Its responsibilities included:

 (i) The formation of short and long-term policy for all types of cooperatives in the country;

 (ii) To work closely with the ruling party and government in all matters pertaining to cooperatives in the country; and

 (iii) Election of a national chairman and committee members who supervised day-to-day operations of the UCS (Act supplement No. 9 of 1979).

The crop authorities and other marketing parastatals were government marketing institutions which had no direct administrative responsibilities in villages and Ujamaa villages but were the only buyers of the farmer's crops which gave them influence and prominence.

Villages depended on the prices offered for crops they delivered to the marketing parastatals and crop authorities and on the services which the crop authorities and parastatals provided to improve the marketing system.

The price for agricultural crops was determined by the cost of production, marketing costs, and the margin which the marketing institutions decided to retain for their existence. Sometimes, political considerations were taken into account to make sure that crop prices were not unnecessarily inflated at the expense of consumers.

The marketing of agricultural products was an important function of village multi-purpose cooperative societies. In Tanzania it included two major categories of crops. The first category was food crops such as maize, wheat, rice, sorghum, coconut, millet, cassava, sugar, and oil seeds (peanuts, sesame, sunflower and castor oil). The second category consisted of Tanzania's major cash crops such as cotton, tea, coffee, sisal, tobacco, cashew nuts, pyrethrum and livestock. Most of these products came from smallholder farming. But there were also state farms for some crops and cattle ranches. All marketed agricultural products, whether for domestic use or for export, and were controlled and/or handled by marketing institutions.

At the village level, the peasants were required to sell their farm products through the village cooperative organization, which bought crops for national institutions for marketing agricultural products. The most important feature of the Tanzania crop marketing system was the compulsory cash crop marketing through the village organization. Virtually all marketed peasants' agricultural products in Tanzania had to be sold through the village organization. This could have resulted in, increased marketing services, lower unit marketing costs, and the elimination of profits since in theory village cooperative members had to receive patronage refunds in case their village cooperative realized a surplus from the cooperative business enterprise. In reality, village members did not receive patronage refunds since national marketing institutions were not cooperatives.

Village multi-purpose cooperatives received funds and either bought directly from their members on behalf of national marketing institutions or they assembled the crops and informed the national marketing institutions to send their employees to the villages to buy the crops. Whether the village organizations bought crops from peasants on behalf of national marketing institutions or employees of the latter came to the villages to buy crops, the village organizations were involved in the marketing process. The village organizations ensured that crops were assembled at village buying posts. The village organizations were also involved in basic grading, weighing, bagging, storage, keeping records of purchases, stocks, consignments, and calculating costing estimates of the business enterprise. In case employees of a national marketing institution came to the villages to buy crops, the village organizations also provided marketing services to ensure that the transactions were executed fairly for both the peasants and national marketing institutions.

The personnel of a village multi-purpose cooperative who dealt with crop selling were:

a) Secretary – organized the collection and handling procedures and exerted general supervision;

b) Treasurer – kept the records and accounts and made cash payments to farmers;

c) Committeemen – checked grading, weights and stocks; and

d) Casual Labourer – moved bags and stocked the produce in stores.

The village multi-purpose cooperative societies were linked directly with the national agricultural marketing institutions. The national marketing institutions had their offices and employees in the regions and districts which produced the crops which they controlled and marketed.

The National Milling Corporation (NMC) was officially recognized as having a national monopoly and monopsony to market food crops such as cereal crops. The NMC bought food crops and sold them in the domestic market and where necessary the NMC exported crops to foreign markets and the imported grains from foreign countries. The General Agricultural Product Export Corporation (GAPEX) was a general purpose agricultural export parastatal which dealt with various cash crops for export.

For each of the export cash crops, marketing was controlled by a Crop Authority such as the Coffee Authority of Tanzania (CAT), the Tobacco Authority of Tanzania (TAT), the Tanzania Cotton Authority (TCA), the Tanzania Tea Authority (TTA), and the Cashew Nut Authority of Tanzania (CATA). A crop authority had exclusive authority to monitor, supervise, direct, and control the whole crop industry from development and production, to marketing. These national institutions for marketing agricultural products advised the government on crop prices. They kept the government informed about the business enterprises of marketing agricultural products (Cooperative College Moshi, 1982: 47).

Conclusion

Marketing cooperatives in Tanzania were very important in the marketing chain for farm products. They received crops which were delivered in the primary societies for sale by farmers. Cooperative Unions received farm products from their primary cooperative societies and sold them to buyers at auctions or exported them to foreign buyers. Marketing cooperatives were organizations in which members could participate in their business enterprises. The marketing cooperatives had experienced successes and failures in their history before they were abolished in 1976.

The implementation of socialism led to the decline of cooperatives. Eventually, the government abolished marketing cooperatives The villagization policy was colliding with the requirement of the Cooperative Societies Act 1968 to register villages as cooperatives. The Villages and Ujamaa Villages Act, 1975 stated that registered villages should function as multi-purpose cooperatives. Cooperative Unions were abolished together with their village primary societies, which were registered under the Cooperative Societies Act, 1968. These could not operate in a village registered under the Village and Ujamaa Villages Act, 1975. The village multipurpose cooperatives had many problems which made them unable to function as cooperatives. The villages sold crops to national marketing institutions which were not cooperatives. Cooperative objectives, principles and practices could not be sufficiently observed in village multi-purpose cooperatives which were registered by the villages and Ujamaa Villages Act, 1975.

References

Banturaki, A., 2000, *The Development of Cooperatives in Tanzania,* Dar es Salaam: Dar es Salaam University Press.

Cliffe, L., Peter Lawrence, William Luttrel, Shem Migbt-Adhola and John S. Saul (eds.), 1975, *Rural Cooperation in Tanzania,* Dar es Salaam: Tanzania Publishing House.

Cooperative College Moshi, 1982, Appropriate Management Systems for Agricultural Cooperation in Tanzania, Management Guide.

Forster, P.G. and Sam Maghimbi (eds.), 1992, *The Tanzanian Peasantry Economy in Crisis,* Aldershot: Ashgate Publishing Ltd..

Hyden, Goran, (ed.), 1976, *Cooperatives in Tanzania: Problems of Organization Building,* Dar es Salaam: Tanzania Publishing House.

International Co-operative Alliance (ICA), 1995, Definition and Principles of a Co-operative, London: International Cooperative Information Centre.

Kimario, A.M., 1992, *Marketing Cooperatives in Tanzania. Problems and Prospects,* Dar es Salaam: Dar es Salaam University Press.

Lyimo F.F., 1983, Peasant Production and Cooperative Experiences in Tanzania: Case studies of villages in Moshi (rural), and Urambo Districts, Ph.D. Dissertation, University of Wisconsin-Madison.

Maghimbi, S., 1990, 'Cooperatives in Agricultural Development' in O'Neil, N. and Mustafa, K. (eds.), 1990, *Capitalism, Socialism and Development Crisis in Tanzania,* Aldershot: Asagate Publishing Ltd., pp. 81-100.

Muungano wa Vyama vya Ushirika Tanganyika, 1977, *Ushirika Wetu,* Dar es Salaam: Printfast.

Nyerere, J.K., 1967, *Freedom and Socialism,* Dar es Salaam: Oxford University Press.

Ofisi ya Waziri Mkuu na Makamu wa Pili wa Rais, 1975, *Sheria ya Kuandikisha Vijiji na Vijiji vya Ujamaa,* Dodoma: Printpak Ltd.

Saul, John S., 'Marketing Cooperative in a Developing Country: The Tanzania case', in Cliffe, Lionel and John S. Saul (eds.), 1972, *Socialism in Tanzania,* Vol. 2 Policies. An Interdisciplinary Reader, Vol. 2, Ch. 54, Dar es Salaam: East African Publishing House.

The United Republic of Tanzania, 2003, *Cooperative Development Policy,* 2002, Dar es Salaam: Government Printer.

United Republic of Tanzania, 1981, Report of the Prime Minister's Commission of Enquiry into the Possibility of Re-establishing Cooperative Unions, Unpublished: Dodoma.

Widstrands, Carl Gosta (ed.), 1970, *Cooperatives and Rural Development in East Africa,* New York: African Publishing Co.

Young, Crawford, Neal P. Sherman and Tim H. Rose, 1981, *Cooperatives and Development. Agricultural Policies in Ghana and Tanzania,* Madison: University of Wisconsin Press.

7

The Re-establishment and Restructuring of Cooperatives

The re-introduction of cooperatives and the restructuring of the cooperative movement in1982 was an important cooperative movement in Tanzania. This chapter first analyzes problems posed by the village cooperative system that was regulated by the Villages and Ujamaa Villages Act, 1975. Second, the report of the Prime Minister's Commission of Enquiry and its recommendations in re-introducing marketing cooperatives are analyzed.[16] The chapter then examines the decision of the government to re-establish cooperatives and restructure the cooperative movement. Finally, the way forward for cooperatives is assessed.

Government parastatals and village governments failed to perform the tasks formerly assigned to the marketing cooperatives. Thus, the cooperative market system collapsed, and the supply of farm inputs and credit was disrupted and even ceased in some villages. This was mainly because government parastatals and villages were inefficient and lacked the business administrative capacity to perform these tasks. Farmers suffered great hardships and the production of major cash and food crops declined substantially. This made it impossible for the country to attain its objectives of improving the economic conditions of farmers and the attainment of self-sufficiency in food production (Kimario, A.M. 1992). The crop authorities continued buying farm products but failed to collect them on time and they also could not provide timely price incentives and farm inputs to improve production.

7.1 Problems of the Village Cooperative System

The abolition of primary cooperatives had negative effects on the economy. The policy makers learned that the village cooperative system was not working as smoothly as expected. Farmers expressed great dissatisfaction with the marketing crop authorities who handled their crops. The main reasons for farmers' dissatisfaction were the reduction of prices paid for all crops handled by the crop authorities, and that crops were in some cases bought on credit and not with cash.

That situation led to low crop production because farmers were less motivated to increase their production. For instance, according to a Marketing Development Bureau report, production of cotton dropped from 100% in 1974/1975 to 68% in 1980 while cashew nuts dropped from 100% in 1974/1975 to 16% in 1982 (Maghimbi in Foster P.G. and Sam Maghimbi (eds.) 1992). Although other factors such as shortage of rain could cause low production levels, the inefficiency of the crop authorities

16 The Prime Minister appointed a commission of Enquiry to study the problems facing Village Multi-purpose Cooperatives and recommend how to re-introduce cooperatives and restructure the Cooperative movement in Tanzania.

contributed much to the situation. As a result, in November 1980 the Prime Minister appointed a committee of enquiry to find the most effective way to overcome the problems. The commission submitted its report in February 1981. The report revealed that the village cooperative system was ineffective because of the following problems:

a) There were legal problems in the Villages Act, 1975. Villages were registered as villages which would function as multipurpose cooperatives, but there were no references to cooperative principles. This lead to serious problems in the villages' cooperative system because villages could not operate under a cooperative identity. This led to other problems including the following:

   (i) Economic activities in villages were not carried out according to the cooperative principles that formed the cornerstone of cooperative business undertakings. Business ventures established by villages, such as farm projects and shops, were identified as village projects and not cooperative businesses;

   (ii) It happened that if more than one village wanted to establish a joint common business, the Villages Act 1975 did not specify how to go about it. This tended to discourage villages from undertaking business ventures which would involve more than one village; and

   (iii) The Villages Act, 1975 did not specify a cooperative body in the village structure which would guide the development of cooperative ventures. The ruling authority in the village council placed more emphasis on the council's party and government responsibilities in the villages rather than on the promotion of cooperative business.

b) There were administrative problems in numerous villages where the administration was purposely simplified in order to reduce costs.

   (i) Most of the villages depended on voluntary or part-time personnel to carry out administrative work. However, the administrative machinery did not have the capacity to cope with the development program as both the party and government anticipated; and

   (ii) Development programs suffered from the misuse of funds because the village cooperative management did not have the capacity to control the expenditures for projects in the villages. Village cooperative management did not have the capacity to control their finances and so suffered funds misuse.

c) Economic problems in village cooperatives occurred as the result of the application of the Village and Ujamaa Villages Act, 1975. This Act stressed the economic development of registered villages so that they could function as multi-purpose cooperatives, but policy makers put more emphasis on the involvement of villagers in village government and party affairs. This emphasis led to the creation of a poor financial base in village multi-purpose Cooperatives and failed to provide villagers with services that were needed to improve agriculture. Villages were also unable to employ full time managers to run their cooperative affairs. If villages employed village managers, it was extremely difficult to pay them monthly salaries as villages were given funds for crop purchases rather than staff salaries; and

d) After the dissolution of Cooperative Unions, crop authorities became the only buyers of crops from villages and as a result there were market operational problems:

   (i) Crops in the villages were not bought on time as sometimes the NMC and crop authorities did not properly prepare themselves to buy crops before the next harvest season, or sometimes they could not buy crops from a certain village at that moment because that time they were dealing with other villages;

   (ii) Crop authorities did not pay farmers on time for crop they purchased. It normally took 3 to 6 months and sometimes up to a year or more for farmers to be paid for their crops. This delayed payment made farmers lose the morale to produce and it also forced them to sell their products to middle men who cheated and exploited them; and

   (iii) Crop authorities sometimes failed to transport crops they had purchased on time and caused the crops to lose their quality which reduced their worth and reduced the earnings of crop authorities (The United Republic of Tanzania, 1981: 5-8, 81).

7.2 Recommendations of the Prime Minister's Commission of Enquiry

The Prime Minister's Commission of Enquiry recommended that the Village and Ujamaa Villages (Registration and Administration) Act, 1975 should be reviewed to allow cooperatives to be formed according to members' needs as stipulated in the cooperative principles and the Cooperative Societies Act, 1968 as the Villages and Ujamaa Villages Act, 1975 was not appropriate or valid to register cooperatives (The United Republic of Tanzania, 1981).

The main recommendation of the Prime Ministers' Commission of Enquiry was the immediate reestablishment of cooperatives (The United Republic of Tanzania 1981: 5-8).

a) Revival of three tier cooperative system

The commission felt that the old three tier cooperative system consisting of primary societies, cooperative unions and National Cooperative organization provided a more efficient marketing channel than the villages and crop authorities. Primary societies should be formed by members from either one or more villages, depending on economic viability and membership in cooperatives should be open and voluntary (The United Republic of Tanzania 1981: 81-82). Cooperative unions could be formed either at the district or regional level depending on economic viability and the needs of members. The main purpose of unions was to strengthen the power of their members. Unions had to incorporate all cooperative activities in their area of operation. That is to say, all cooperative societies at the grassroots level had to affiliate themselves with a union. Therefore, in order to cater for the needs of members, the cooperative unions had the following tasks:

(i) Securing funds for crop finance;
(ii) Transportation of produce from primary societies;
(iii) Distribution of inputs to affiliated societies;
(iv) Processing of agricultural produce to increase its quality;
(v) Provision of technical advice to members; and
(vi) Representation of primary societies at regional and national levels.

The National Cooperative Organization could be formed by district and regional cooperative unions and operate under the Cooperative Societies Act, 1968 rather than the Villages Act, 1975, which didn't provide an ideal environment for the promotion and development of viable rural cooperatives. The apex organization was to deal with the following tasks:

(i) Establishing man-power requirements of the cooperative movement;
(ii) Giving expert advice on employment policy and regulations;
(iii) Encouraging cooperative unions and societies to establish education and training funds; and
(iv) Advising the unions, societies, the cooperative college, and the government on training matters.

b) The commission recommended the establishment and strengthening of the following to provide maximum support to the cooperative movement:

   (i) Cooperative bank to take care of the financial requirements of the cooperative movement and was to be owned by the movement itself. The bank would provide loans for recurrent expenditure on crop purchase and production activities.

   (ii) Cooperative colleges and education centers to carry out comprehensive education and training programs for members, committees, and the general public. They also had to provide effective relevant training to staff employed in the cooperative movement.

c) Other recommendations by the Prime Minister's commission of enquiry were the following:

   (i) All assets which were taken over by crops authorities from the unions and primary societies in 1976 had to be paid fully according to their determined value. If for any reasons crop authorities were unable to pay, government should pay on their behalf;

   (ii) The National Milling Corporation and crop authorities had to pay rent for houses and other properties belonging to cooperatives that they had been using since 1976;

   (iii) All claims from the National Bank of Commerce on interest for overdrafts which were taken by Cooperative Unions before their dissolution in 1976 would be directed to the crop authorities because the unions were out of business from that year, or alternatively the claims would be written off; and

   (iv) All assets which had been taken over by the National Milling Corporation and crop authorities but which could still be utilized would be handed back to the respective unions and primary societies (The United Republic of Tanzania, 1981).

7.3 Government Decision to Re-establish Cooperatives

The government accepted the commission's report and prepared a paper outlining its stand on re-establishing the Regional Cooperative Unions and structuring the cooperative movement.

The government formally announced the re-introduction of cooperative unions and primary cooperative societies in 1982. This was stated more clearly in the final report of the Tanzania National Agriculture Policy, produced by the Ministry of Agriculture in 1982, that cooperative unions should be re-established to take over the majority of the services carried out by the crop authorities (Maghimbi in Foster, G and Sam Maghimbi (eds) 1992).

The Tanzanian government responded to the recommendations proposed by the Prime Minister's Commission of Enquiry into the possibility of re-establishing cooperative societies and unions. As an outcome the government enacted the Cooperative Societies Act, 1982. According to the Act, the organizational set-up of the cooperative movement in Tanzania consisted of primary societies, cooperative unions, and National Cooperative organization (United Republic of Tanzania, 1982).

The Cooperative Societies Act, 1982 repealed and replaced the Cooperative Societies Act, 1968. The government split the former Ujamaa, Cooperative and Rural Development Division into departments of Cooperative Development and Community Development (Cooperative College, Moshi. May, 1982: 40-41). The Act provided for the formation, constitution, registration and the functioning of Cooperative Societies as instruments for the implementation of the Policy of Socialism and Self-Reliance. (Taylor and Mackenzie, 1992). Section 15 of the Act made provision for a structure of cooperative societies at three levels: primary

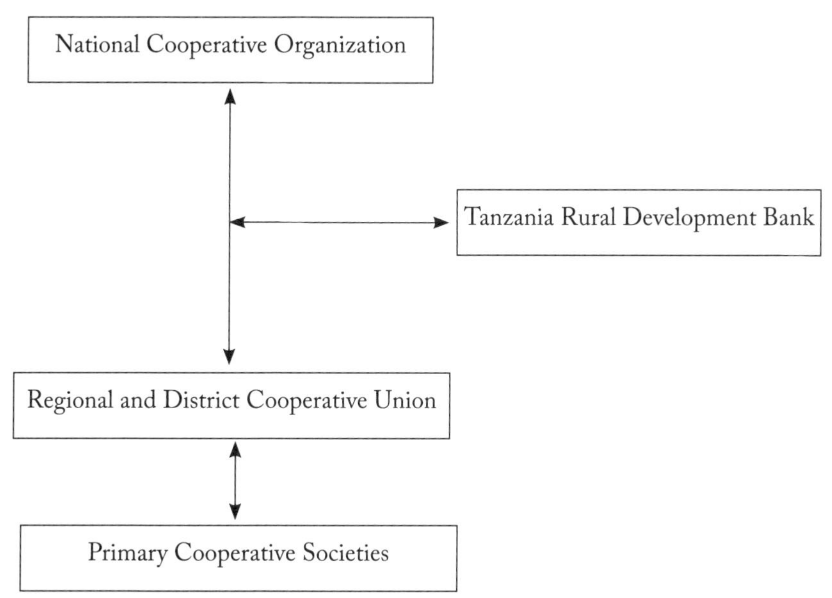

Fig. 4 Organizational Structure of Agricultural Cooperatives in Accordance with the Cooperative Societies Act, 1982

society, secondary society and the National Cooperative (Fig. 4). Ten or more people could form a primary cooperative society. A primary society could be formed in a village where it was economically viable; otherwise it could be formed for two or more villages as determined by the Registrar of cooperatives. A cooperative Union could be formed for a region and where it was more economically viable; it could with the approval of the Minister, be formed in a district or districts. At the national level the National Cooperative organization had to provide, organize and supervise services to member societies (United Republic of Tanzania, 1982).

The Cooperative Societies Act, 1982, Section 22, stated that every rural cooperative society should be a multi-purpose society, and Section 23 specified that no cooperative society other than a rural cooperative society could operate within a village.17 The Act stipulated that residents in a village and who had a specialized skill relevant to a specific trade could organize themselves into a cooperative group for the purpose of pursuing that trade. The Act also stipulated that a cooperative group had to operate as a specialized line of production and had to perform their functions as a specialized branch of the rural cooperative development committee (United Republic of Tanzania 1982(a) Section 23(2)).

Membership of a rural cooperative society was granted to any person who attained the age of 18 years and was a resident of the village, owned land, and was following a trade or an occupation relevant to the primary society's objects within its area of operation (Cooperative Societies Act, 1992(24)). A cooperative development committee should be elected for every rural cooperative society in accordance with the provisions of Cooperative Societies Act. The cooperative development committee had to be elected by the general assembly (Cooperative Societies Act, 1982 (25)).

The Tanzania Rural Development Bank (amendment) Act, 1982 enabled cooperatives to align the bank's activities more towards rural development. Under the Tanzania Rural Development Bank (TRDB) (amendment) Act, 1982, Primary and Secondary Cooperative Societies could acquire shares in the TRDB through the National Cooperative organization. In this way, cooperative societies could benefit more from TRDB loans for crops, and other rural development financing possibilities.

---

17 A rural area is any area within the jurisdiction of a village, and a Rural Cooperative society is a society which is formed in a rural area (Cooperative Societies Act, 1982 Section 3).

The Cooperative Audit and Supervision Act, 1982 established the Cooperative Audit and Supervision Corporation which provided audit and supervision services to all registered cooperative societies.

The re-established cooperatives were much weaker than those predating 1976, and they suffered from obstructive and ineffective government policies and structural adjustment programs. A cooperative society had to strive, in accordance with its democratic, socialist, and cooperative outlook to achieve the following objectives:

a) To accelerate the fostering of socialism and bring about socialist development both in rural and urban areas;

b) To foster the development of cooperative farming in rural areas as a means of modernizing and developing agriculture and eliminating exploitation in the rural areas;

c) To satisfy the cultural needs of its members as well as increase their social and political welfare; and

d) To improve the material living conditions of its members (United Republic of Tanzania, 1982(a) Section 5).

By 1984, the cooperative movement had been re-established. The National Milling Corporation (NMC) surrendered its operations in districts to cooperative unions and confined itself to its regional headquarters. Regional Trading Companies (RTC) also surrendered their businesses in the districts to cooperative unions although some of the shops were established by the RTC's themselves and not inherited from the abolished unions. Crop Authorities were transformed into marketing boards that bought crops from cooperatives Unions, which were reassuming their former functions of buying products from primary cooperative societies. 1982 to 1984 was a period of cooperative re-establishment. This meant the relinquishing of a considerable amount of centralized government control over produce marketing to cooperative organizations as a whole. People were demanding the structural reform of local marketing organizations which were to become independent organizations so they could meet their needs. They demanded democratic management and control by cooperatives' membership. The government policy on cooperatives since 1991 has been explicit in its three aims. Firstly, it has sought to ensure the institutionalization and implementation of the basic cooperative principles and structural development of genuine cooperative enterprise. Secondly, to ensure capacity building in cooperatives in view of achieving member empowerment and, a higher degree of efficiency and effectiveness. Thirdly, to ensure that government created an environment in which cooperatives could conduct their activities with efficiency and effectiveness as befitting the true characteristics of democratic and autonomous cooperative organizations.

The government put a program (1992-1999) for developing the cooperative movement. Following the 1991 Cooperative Legislation (URT 1991), it was envisaged that government and political interactions would end, and cooperatives would reform themselves. Cooperatives Reform Program was divided into two phases. Phase One of the Reform Program (1992 – 1994) was for the institutionalization and implementation of basic cooperative principles and for the structural development of genuine cooperative enterprises. The government was required in the first phase to set up the model for the restructuring process whereby rural cooperatives were to be reformed (based on economic viability criteria, cooperative principles, and sound practice). Phase Two (1995 – 1999) of the reform program dealt with capacity building for the cooperative movement in order to achieve member empowerment and higher degrees of efficiency and effectiveness (URT 1991).

The newly formed multipurpose cooperatives were based on one or more villages according to their economic viability. This reduced the number of registered cooperatives substantially from 8,100 in 1981 to 1,945 in November 1985. This made it administratively simpler to provide supervisory and technical support. Out of almost 2000 primary cooperatives registered between 1982 and 1986, there were 323 cooperatives societies based on single villages. The primary cooperatives collected products from members, graded, and weighed and put them in stores until they were marketed through the unions to the respective marketing boards, and passed on payment from the unions to individual members through their cooperative societies. According to the Cooperative Act 1982, all cooperative unions had to operate regionally rather than at district level to make them economically viable and administratively manageable (URT 1982(a)).

The re-establishment of cooperative unions and primary societies in Tanzania was a great achievement for farmers in general and co-operators in particular. When cooperatives were re-introduced in 1982, they had lost their monopoly in buying peasants' crops in their respective areas and had to compete with crop merchants. The structural adjustment policies had weakened the cooperatives to the extent that they could not buy all crops as they had been doing before they were abolished in 1976 (URT 1982 (d)).

These changes are evidence that cooperatives as a tool of development could not be easily replaced by other forms of organization. The significance of cooperatives therefore, lied not only in providing specific social and economic benefits to its members but also in their sensitivity and readiness to respond to the total needs and aspirations of their patrons. This was indeed the reason why peasants in Tanzania felt they had missed an important link in their social and economic lives as a result of the abolition of the marketing cooperatives in 1976.

7.4 Persistent Problems in the Re-established Cooperatives

Cooperative members were concerned about the clarity of the Cooperative Societies Act, 1982 on issues of open membership, shared contributions, and the freedom of members to form cooperatives of their own choice at a the village level. The government did not fully implement the recommendations of the Prime Minister's Commission of Enquiry. The Commission of Enquiry recommended re-establishing cooperatives using the Cooperative Societies Act, 1968 but the government instead enacted the Cooperative Societies Act, 1982, which re-structured the cooperative movement to accelerate the implementation of socialism and bringing about socialist development both in rural and urban areas. The Cooperative Societies Act, 1982 increased the powers of the government and party at the expense of members' democratic control thus reducing their autonomy drastically. Likewise, there was discouragement in forming other types of cooperatives in areas of operation by rural multipurpose cooperatives (URT 1982(a)) even though such actions would be for the benefit of members.

The process of re-establishing and restructuring the cooperatives was not carried out smoothly, and the cooperatives faced various problems: firstly, there were financial problems such as those faced during the 1980s, when the government depended on the agriculture sector as the main source of national income. More than 70% of the population lived in rural areas and practiced agriculture, which provided more than 80% of the Gross National Product (GNP). Following the abolition of marketing cooperatives and their replacement by state marketing corporations and crop authorities, there was a decline in peasant farm produce available for sale to domestic and foreign markets.

Secondly, cooperatives normally paid farmers an advance against revenues during delivery of products at the buying centers and final payments only after products had been sold and operational costs had been deducted from the revenue accrued. The introduction of the new cooperatives came with the policy of trade liberalization, such that peasants could sell their farm products wherever they preferred, so that from 1985 on peasants were selling to middlemen who bought on a cash basis.

Thirdly, the new regional cooperative unions had transport problems which made it difficult for them to go to the primary cooperative society's stores on time to move products to their This led to delays making final payments to peasants through their cooperative societies.

Fourth, when the cooperatives were re-established, they did not fill the administrative and managerial positions in the cooperatives with qualified staff or faithful leaders. Several cases were reported to police and courts concerning the stealing of money and cooperative properties as well as the making of ghost payments.

Fifth, there were operating problems in cooperative unions. By May 2001, cooperatives in Tanzania owed banks Tsh. 17.8 billion. This was very discouraging because cooperatives had accumulated this debt despite the cancellation of Tsh. 44 billion in debts by the government in the 1990s. This was revealed during the general meeting of the Arusha Cooperative Union (ACU) on June 23, 2001. The ACU itself owed banks more than Tsh. 5.8 billion and it owed other creditors Tsh. 899 million (Daily News 25 June, 2001: 07).

Sixth, there were weaknesses in staffing capacity in different governmental institutions responsible for cooperative development under the Ministry of Agriculture and Cooperatives, such as in the Cooperative Department in charge of supervision of the implementation of laws and policies and Cooperative auditing.

Seventh, many cooperative members were not well informed about cooperatives because most of them had not received enough education about cooperative to the extent that some members did not even know their rights and responsibilities.

Eighth, new economic policies of trade liberalization allowed businessmen to conduct free trade, which affected cooperatives. Collecting crops from individual households instead of at the cooperative centres led to poor crop grading, and affected the price of crops due to cheating in weighing and pricing.

The special committee appointed by President Benjamin W. Mkapa in 2000 to investigate and recommend what could be done to rejuvenate the cooperative sector reported that the movement had been suffering from a lack of capital, unstable bureaucratic structures, problems of leadership, misappropriation and theft (Wizara ya Ushirika na Masoko, 2001).

Most cooperatives failed to provide loans to members and they did not offer proper prices for peasants' crops. Also most services provided by cooperatives before 1976 were no longer provided as of 2001, so peasants did not believe in the capacity of cooperatives to help them. As a result, members cancelled their membership. The entire cooperative movement had only 55,248 members. The average was 107 per cooperative which was 20% of the average membership in a cooperative before cooperatives were abolished in 1976 when the average was 549 members per cooperative (Wizara ya Ushirika na Masoko 2001: 21). Another problem was the lack of funds due to economic policies like the privatization of various institutions. This is because the government was no longer a trustee for cooperatives wishing to secure loans from banks.

There were constraints which faced cooperatives in Tanzania:

a) The main constraint was the inability of cooperatives to operate under a liberalized economy. Within the free market economy cooperatives were weak structurally and financially;

b) Another constraint was the weak institutional foundation which gave little emphasis to full democracy and ownership by members. Some primary cooperatives sold crops to private traders and rented out their facilities to them. There was also a problem with the misappropriation of cooperative society resources by dishonest managers and management committee members; and

c) The lack of training for members on cooperative principles and practices (The United Republic of Tanzania, 2003: 2-3).

7.5 The Way Forward for Cooperatives

The Cooperative Development Policy, 2002 and the Cooperative Societies Act, 2003 and their future improvements are guiding documents on which to base efforts to strengthen cooperatives in Tanzania. Cooperative policy and legislation must strictly abide and comply with the principles of cooperatives, which will make cooperatives valid and reliable as business organizations that are member-centered.

Member education should be intensified to increase member awareness and consciousness about cooperatives. Education and training should also be provided to cooperative members, leaders and staff. It would be beneficial to introduce cooperative studies, starting in primary schools, planning and implementing special programmes for cooperative education for the public, and budgeting special funds for cooperative education. Management training can improve the performance of management staff of cooperatives.

Making essential cooperative services available to their members, especially in the form of the provision of farm inputs, farm credit, cooperative loans, farm services, and marketing services are necessary to induce more people to become cooperative members. Vertical integration and concentration of service and inputs with a high scientific and technological capability would bring rapid and huge positive changes which would make cooperatives effective in modernizing farming, fishing, mining and other cooperative activities.

Cooperation between and among cooperatives might be useful for cooperatives to share and exchange cooperative experiences. Small and new cooperatives in particular, could be assisted by larger established cooperatives. Expertise along with technical and technological differences could be shared, learned and borrowed from a more advanced and better-equipped cooperative.

7.6 Cooperative Vision and Mission

The vision of a future Tanzanian Cooperative system is geared towards improved and sustainable cooperatives that are capable of fulfilling members' economic and social needs (The United Republic of Tanzania, 2003(b): 5).

The Cooperative Mission is to develop Cooperatives that are:

a) Owned and Controlled by their members;
b) Work for the betterment of members' own economic and social development and that of the community in which they live;
c) Operate competitively as independent economic entities; and
d) Care for the present and future members (The United Republic of Tanzania, 2003(b): 6-7).

Conclusion

The re-establishment and restructuring of the cooperative movement in 1982 was an important government action in the history of cooperatives in Tanzania. The decision to re-establish the cooperatives followed the recommendations of the Prime Minister's Commission of Enquiry in 1981. (United Republic of Tanzania, 1981). The Prime Minister's Commission of Enquiry found that the Village Cooperative which were registered using Villages and Ujamaa villages Act 1975 failed in Cooperative development in Tanzania. The current Cooperative Societies Act, 2003 and the Cooperative Development Policy (United Republic of Tanzania (2003 (b)) are instrumental for strengthening the cooperatives and expanding the cooperative movement.

Government help is required by cooperatives in terms of training cooperative staff and members, auditing cooperative accounts and license and tax laws favoring cooperatives to at least help them develop into self-sustaining entities. Lastly, intensive research should be conducted before establishing cooperatives and legal action should also be taken against leaders and cooperative staff on theft and corrupt practices.

References

Andrew, Bibby, 2006, *Standing on their own two feet, Cooperative Reform in Tanzania,* Dar es Salaam: International Labour Organization.

Banturaki, J.A., 2000, *Cooperative and Poverty Alleviation*, Dar es Salaam: Tema Publishers.

Cooperative College, Moshi, 1982, Appropriate Management Systems for Agricultural Copoperation in Tanzania, Unpublished: Management Guide.

Forster, Peter G. and Sam Maghimbi (eds.), 1999, *Agrarian Economy, State and Society in Contemporary Tanzania,* Aldershot: Ashgate Publishing Ltd.

Forster, Peter G. and Sam Maghimbi (eds.), 1992, *The Tanzanian Peasantry: Economy in Crisis*, Aldershot: Ashgate Publishing Ltd.

Kimario, A.M., 1992, *Marketing Cooperatives in Tanzania. Problems and Prospects,* Dar es Salaam: Dar es Salaam University Press.

Lyimo F.F, 1983, Peasant Production and Cooperative Experiences in Tanzania: Case studies of villages in Moshi (rural), and Urambo Districts, Ph.D. Dissertation, University of Wisconsin-Madison.

Msambichaka, 1985, An Appraisal of 1984-85, Agricultural Policies on Pricing Subsidies, and exchange rate in Tanzania, Unpublished.

Ponte, S., 2002, *Farmers and Markets in Tanzania,* Dar es Salaam: Mkuki na Nyota Publishers.

Tungaraza, F., Mchomvu A. and Sam Maghimbi, 2002, 'Social Security Systems in Tanzania' in *Journal of Social Development in Africa,* Vol. 17: 2.

Tylor, F & Mackenzie, 1992, *Development From Within: Survival in Rural Africa,* London: Routledge.

United Republic of Tanzania (URT), 2003(b), *Cooperative Development Policy, 2002,* Dar es Salaam: The Government Printer.

United Republic of Tanzania (URT), 1982 (d), *Structural Adjustment Program for Tanzania,* Dar es Salaam: Ministry of Planning and Economic Affairs.

United Republic of Tanzania (URT), 1991, *Cooperative Society Act 1991,* Dar es Salaam: Government Printer.

United Republic of Tanzania (URT), 1981, Report of the Prime Minister's Commission of Enquiry into the Possibility of Re-establishing Cooperative Unions Dodoma, Unpublished.

United Republic of Tanzania (URT), 1982(a), *Cooperative. Societies Act 1982,* Dar es Salaam: Government Printer.

United Republic of Tanzania (URT), 1982(c), *The Cooperative Audit and Supervision Act 1982,* Dar es Salaam: Government Printer.

United Republic of Tanzania (URT), 1982(b), *The Tanzania Rural Development Bank (Amandment) Act, 1982,* Dar es Salaam: Government Printer.

United Republic of Tanzania (URT), 2003(a), The Cooperative Societies Act Number 20 of 2003, Dar es Salaam: Government Printer.

United Republic of Tanzania (URT), 2004, The Cooperative Societies Rules of 2004, Dar es Salaam: Government Printer.

Wizara ya Ushirika na Masoko, 2001, *Taarifa ya Kamati Maalumu ya Rais ya Kumshauri juu ya kufufua, kuimarisha na kuendeleza ushirika Tanzania.* Dar es Salaam: Dar es Salaam University Press.

8

Cooperative Legislations

This chapter analyzes the cooperative legislations applied in the Tanzanian mainland since 1932. The first cooperative ordinance that was the foundation of later cooperative acts is examined. Thereafter follows scrutiny of ordinances and acts that amended, repealed, and replaced subsequent cooperative acts, noting in particular specific legal changes that were made.

Historical precedents laid the foundation for the successive legislations, beginning with the Rochadale Equitable Pioneers Society. This society formulated a set of organizational and working rules. The rules were guidelines based on their experiences. The Rochdale principles, as stated in Chapter Two, were open membership, democratic control, limited interest on shares, patronage rebates, goods to be sold on current market rate and for cash, sale of pure and unadulterated goods, neutrality in religion and politics, and lastly, the continuous education of its members. In 1937, the 5th Congress of the International Cooperative Alliance (ICA) held in Paris, recognized and approved four of the eight principles mentioned above, namely open membership, democratic control, limited interest on shares, and patronage rebates (Sekirasa, Z.I. 1992: 4).

Before the establishment of cooperative societies in Tanganyika, there was a need for the enactment of a cooperative legislation through which cooperative societies were to be formed and operated. Although cooperative ideas were already applied in running the Kilimanjaro Native Planters Association (KNPA, established in 1925), the association was not registered as cooperative society.

8.1 Cooperative Societies Ordinance, No.7 of 1932

8.1.1

In 1931, Mr. C.F. Strickland, Registrar of Cooperatives in Punjab, India, came to Tanzania to advise the government on how to promote cooperatives, and, how to determine appropriate legislation governing their existence. This would allow the growth of a viable cooperative movement under the social and economic conditions prevalent in the country then. Mr. Strickland's recommendations were embodied in the Cooperative Societies Ordinance of March 1932.

8.1.2 Interpretation of Terms

a) 'By-law' means a rule made by a local authority to regulate its own affairs;

b) 'Committee' means the governing body of a registered society to whom the management of its affairs is entrusted;

c) 'Member' includes a person or registered society joining in the application for the registration of a society, and a person or registered society admitted by membership after registration in accordance with the by-laws and rules; and

d) 'Officer' includes a chairman, secretary, treasurer, member of committee, or other person empowered under a society's rules or by-laws to give directions in regard to the business of a registered society. (Cooperative Societies Ordinance, 1932 Section 1.)

8.1.3 Cooperatives' obligation to be registered under the ordinance

The Governor was required to appoint a Registrar of cooperatives for the territory and could appoint Assistant Registrars if necessary, who acted under the control of the Registrar and who observed all the powers of the registrar under this ordinance (Cooperative Societies Ordinance, 1932 Section 3).

Subject to the provisions hereinafter contained, a society which had as its objects the promotion of the economic interests of its members in accordance with cooperative principles, or a society established for the purpose of facilitating the operation of such societies, was supposed to be registered under the ordinance with or without limited liability.

Provided that unless the Governor, by general or special order, otherwise directed:

a) The liability of a society of which a member was a registered society had to be limited; and

b) The liability of a society for which the primary objective was the creation of funds to be loaned to its members, and of which the majority of the members were the agriculturalists and of which no member was registered society, had to be unlimited (Cooperative Ordinance, 1932 Section 4).

c) No member, other than a registered society could hold more than one fifth of the share capital of any cooperative society (Cooperative Ordinance, 1932 Section 5).

d) No society other than a society of which a member was a registered society, could be registered under this ordinance if it did not consist of at least ten persons who had attained their majority and where the objective of the society was the creation of funds to be loaned to its members, unless such persons:

   (i) Resided in the same town, or village, or in the same group of villages; or

(ii) Saved where the registrar otherwise directed were members of the same ethnic group, class, or occupation; and

e) The word limited had to be the last word in the name of every society with limited liability registered under the ordinance (Cooperative Ordinance, 1932 Section 6).

8.1.4 *Rights and Liability of Members*

No member of a registered society could exercise the rights of a member unless, or until he had made such payment to the society in respect of membership or acquired such interests in the society as might be prescribed by the rules or by-laws (Cooperative Ordinance, 1932 Section 12).

Each member of a cooperative society had one vote only as a member in the affairs of the society; provided that a cooperative society, which was a member of any other cooperative society, it could have as many votes as could be prescribed by the by-laws of this other society and could, subject to such, appoint any number of its members, not exceeding the number of such votes, to exercise its voting power (Cooperative Ordinance, 1932 Section 14).

8.1.5 *Duties of Registered Societies*

Every registered society had to have an address registered in accordance with the rules to which all notices and communications could be sent. The society also had to send to the Registrar notice of every change thereof. (Cooperative Ordinance, 1932 Section 16). Every registered society had to keep a copy of the ordinance and of the rules and of its by-laws open to inspection at no cost, at all reasonable times (Cooperative Ordinance, 1932, Section 17).

a) The Registrar had to audit or cause to be audited by some person authorized by him by general or special order in writing in this behalf the accounts of every registered society once at least every year;

b) The audit under sub-section (1) could include an examination of overdue debts if any, and a valuation of the assets and liabilities of the society;

c) The Registrar, the district office, or any person authorized by general or special order in writing in this behalf by the Registrar could at all times have access to all books, accounts, papers, and securities of the society, and every officer of that society had to furnish such information in regard to the transactions and working of the society as the person making such inspection required; and

d) The Registrar and every other person appointed to audit the accounts of a society had power when necessary:
   (i) To summon at the time of his audit any officer, agent, servant, or member of the society, who he had reason to believe could give valuable information in regard to any transactions of the society or the management of its affairs; or
   (ii) To require the production of any book or document relating to the affairs of, or any cash or securities belonging to the society by the officer, agent, servant, or member in possession of such book, document, cash, or securities. (Cooperative Ordinance 1932, Section 18).

8.1.6 Privileges of Registered Societies

The registration of a society rendered it a body corporate by the name under which it was registered, with perpetual succession and a common seal, and with power to hold movable and immovable property of every description, to enter into contracts, to institute and defend suits and other legal proceedings, and to do all things necessary for the purpose of its constitution (Cooperative Ordinance 1932, Section 19).

Subject to the prior claims of the government on the property of its debtors and of landlords in respect of rent, or any money recoverable as rent, a registered society had a first charge.

a) Upon the crops or other agricultural produce of a member or past member, at any time within two years from the date when seed or manure was advanced, or money was lent to such member or past member in respect of the unpaid portion of such advance or loans;
b) In respect of the supply of cattle, fodder for cattle, agriculture or industrial implements or machinery or raw material for manufacture, or of the loan of money for the purchase of any of the foregoing animals or things so supplied or purchased in whole or in part from any such loan or on any articles manufactured from raw materials supplied or purchased (Cooperative Ordinance, 1932 Section 20).

A registered society could have a charge upon the shares or interest in the capital and on the deposits of a member or past member and upon any dividend, bonus, or accumulated funds payable to a member or past member in respect of any debt due from such member or past member to the society, or past member in, or, towards payment of any such debt (Cooperative Ordinance, 1932 Section 21).

8.1.7 *Property and Funds of Registered Societies*

a) A registered society could not grant a loan to any person other than a member. However, provided that, with the general or special sanction of the Registrar, a registered society could make loans to another registered society;

b) Save with the sanction of the Registrar, a society with unlimited liability could not lend money or the security of movable property; and

c) The governor could by general or special order prohibit or restrict the lending of money on a charge of immovable property or any kind thereof by any registered society or class of registered society (Cooperative Ordinance, 1932 Section 31).

d) A registered society could receive deposits and loans from persons who were not members only to such extent, and under such condition, as could be prescribed by the by-laws (Cooperative Ordinance, 1932 Section 32).

e) Save as provided in Sections 31 and 32, the transactions of a registered society with persons other than members had to be subject to such prohibitions and restrictions, if any, as the Governor of Tanganyika could by rules prescribe. (Cooperative Ordinance, 1932 Section 33).

f) A registered society could invest or deposit its funds:

   (i) In the Post Office Savings Bank.

   (ii) In any government Securities approved by the Registrar.

   (iii) In the shares of any other registered society.

   (iv) With any bank or person carrying on the business of banking approved for this purpose by the Registrar.

   (v) In any other mode permitted by the rules. (Cooperative Ordinance, 1932 Section 34).

g) A registered society, having as one of its objectives the disposal of any produce of agriculture, animal husbandry, or handcraft could contract with its members either in its by-laws or by a separate document. Members could dispose of all their produce, or of such amounts or descriptions as might be stated therein, to or through the society. Members could in the contract provide for payment of a specific sum per unit of weight or other measure as liquidated for infringement of the contract, and such sum could be a debt due to the society.

(i) Any such contract could create in favor of the society a first charge upon all produce mentioned therein, whether existing or future, in order to secure the due marketing of the same in accordance with the contract.

(ii) The covenants or obligations imposed by the contract had to be with any lands, buildings, or other structures mentioned therein, and had to be binding on all assignees and transferees, and any transfer or conveyance of property subject to such a contract had to be deemed to operate also as a like transfer or assignment of the contract and of all shares which had been issued in respect of the contract (Cooperative Ordinance, 1932 Section 35).

h) (i) No society could pay a dividend or bonus or distribute any part of its accumulated funds before the balance sheet had been certified by an auditor approved by the Registrar;

(ii) No society could pay a dividend to its members exceeding 10 percent; and

(iii) No society could, with unlimited liability which advances money or goods to any member in excess of money or goods deposited by him, pay a dividend before ten years from the date of its registration (Cooperative Ordinance, 1932 Section 37).

i) (i) Every society which did or could derive a profit from its transactions had to maintain a reserve fund;

(ii) A society with unlimited liability, which advanced money or goods to any member in excess of money or goods deposited by him, could carry one-fourth of the net balance in each year to a reserve fund; and

(iii) All other societies had to carry to the reserve fund such portion of the net balance in each year as could be prescribed by the rules and by-laws (Cooperative Ordinance, 1932 Section 38).

8.1.8 Inspection of affairs

a) The Registrar could of his own motion and upon the request of the district officer, or the application of a majority of the committee, or of not less than one third of the members, hold an inquiry or direct some person authorized by him by written order to act on his behalf to hold an inquiry into the constitution, working and financial condition of a registered society; and

b) All officers and members of the society had to produce the books and documents of the society and furnish such information in regard to the affairs of the society as the registrar or the person authorized by the register would require (Cooperative Ordinance, 1932 Section 41).

The Registrar could on the application of a creditor of a registered society inspect or direct some person authorized by him by written order, to act on his behalf to inspect the books of the society:

Provided that:

a) The applicant satisfied the Registrar that the debt was a sum then due, and that he had demanded payment thereof and had not received satisfaction within a reasonable time; and
b) The applicant deposited with the Registrar such sum as security for the costs of the proposed inspection as the Registrar would require.

The registrar had to communicate the results of any such inspection to the creditor. (Cooperative Ordinance, 1932 Section 42).

Where an inquiry was held, the Registrar could, by a certificate under his hand and seal, make an award apportioning the costs, or such part of the cost as he could think right, between the society, the members or creditor demanding an inquiry or inspection, and the officers or former officers of the society (Cooperative Ordinance, 1932 Section 43).

Any sum awarded by way of costs could be recovered, or production of the certificate referred to the court having jurisdiction over the person from whom the money is claimable, by distress and sale of any movable property belonging to such person within the limits of the jurisdiction of such court, notwithstanding that the sum awarded could be in excess of the ordinary jurisdiction of such court (Cooperative Ordinance, 1932 Section 44).

8.1.9 Dissolution of the Society

a) If the Registrar after an inquiry had been held under section 41, or after an inspection had been made under section 42, or on receipt of an application made by three-fourths of the members of a registered society, was of the opinion that the society ought to be dissolved, he could cancel the registration of that society.
b) Any member of a society could within two months from the date of an order made under sub-section (i) appeal against such an order to the Governor.
c) Where no appeal was presented within two months from the making of an order cancelling the registration of a society, the order could take effect on the expiry of that period.

d) Where an appeal was presented within two months, the order could not take effect until it was confirmed by the Governor of Tanganyika.

e) Where the registrar cancelled registration of a society under sub-section (i), he could make an order as he deemed fit respecting the custody of the books, documents and the protection of the assets of the society until the order canceling the registration of the society took effect (Cooperative Ordinance, 1932 Section 45).

Where it was a condition of the registration of a society that it should consist of at least ten members, the registrar could, by written order, cancel the registration of the society if at any time it was proved to his satisfaction that the number of members had been reduced to less than ten. (Cooperative Ordinance, 1932 Section 46).

Where the registration of a society was cancelled, the society had to cease to exist as a corporate body:

a) In the case of cancellation in accordance with the provision of section 45, from the date the order of cancellation took effect; and

b) In the case of cancellation in accordance with the provisions of section 46, from the date of the order (Cooperative Ordinance, 1932 Section 47).

8.1.10 Rules

a) The Governor in council could, for any registered society or class of such societies, make rules to carry out the purposes of the ordinance.

b) In particular and without prejudice to the generality of the foregoing power, such rules could:

   (i) Subject to the provisions of section 5, prescribe the maximum number of shares or portion of the capital of a society which could be held by a member;

   (ii) Prescribe the forms to be used and the conditions to be complied with in the making of applications for the registration of a society and the procedure in the matter of such applications;

   (iii) Prescribe the matters in respect to which a society could make by-laws and for the procedure to be followed in making, altering, and abrogating by-laws, and the conditions to be satisfied prior to such making, alteration or abrogation;

   (iv) Prescribe the conditions to be complied with by persons applying for admission or admitted as members and provide for the election and admission of members, and the payment to be made and the interests to be acquired before the exercise of the right of membership;

(v) Regulate the manner in which funds could be raised by means of shares, or debenture, or otherwise, and the form in which any application for financial assistance from the government could be made;

(vi) Provide for general meeting of the members and for the procedure and the powers to be exercised by such meetings;

(vii) Provide for the appointment, suspension, and removal of members of the committee and other officers, and for the procedures at committee meetings, the powers to be exercised and the duties to be performed by members and other officers;

(viii) Provide for an audit of the accounts and books to be kept by a society and the charges, if any, to be made for such an audit;

(ix) Provide for the periodical publication of a balance sheet showing the assets and liabilities of a society;

(x) Provide for the persons by whom, and the form in which copies of entities in books of societies could be certified;

(xi) Provide for the formation and maintenance of a register of members and, where the liability of members is limited by shares, of the register of shares;

(xii) Provided that any dispute touching the business of a society between members or past members of the society, or persons claiming through a member or past member, or between a member or past member or persons so claiming and the committee or any officer, could be referred to the Registrar for a decision or, if the Registrar so directed, to arbitration under the Arbitration Ordinance, 1931; and

(xiii) In any case where the Registrar was satisfied that a substantial number of members of any society were unacquainted with the English language, he could cause such rules to be translated into a language with which such members are acquainted, and additionally to be made known in such a manner as is customary for the community concerned (Cooperative Ordinance, 1932 Section 50).

8.1.11 Offences

a) It would be an offence under this ordinance if:

(i) A society or an officer or a member thereof willfully neglected or refused to do any act or to furnish any information required for the purpose of this ordinance by the Registrar or other person duly authorized by him/her in writing;

(ii) A society, or an officer, or member thereof, willfully made a false return or furnished false information;

(iii) Any person who willfully, or without any reasonable excuse, disobeyed any summons requisition, or lawful written order issued under the provisions of this ordinance, or did not furnish any information lawfully required from him by a person authorized to do so under the provisions of this ordinance; and

b) Every society, officer, or member of a society or other person guilty of an offence under this section would be liable to a fine not exceeding five hundred shillings. (Cooperative Ordinance, 1932 Section 53).

Any person, firm or company having knowledge or notice or the existence of a contract described in section 35 of an obligation upon producers, who solicited or persuaded any person to sell or deliver produce in violation of that contract or obligation could be liable to fine of five hundred shillings for each offence, and could in addition be required to pay to the society concerned the market price of such produce as at the date of such offence (Cooperative Ordinance, 1932 Section 54).

a) No person other than a registered society could trade or carry on business under any name, or title, of which the word 'cooperative' or its equivalent in any other language was part, without the sanction of the Governor of Tanganyika; and

b) Whoever contravened the provisions of this section could on convictions be punishable with a fine not exceeding two hundred shillings and in case of a continuing offence, with a further fine of fifty shillings for each day of which the offence is continued after conviction (Cooperative Ordinance, 1932 Section 55).

The Governor could by general or special order, exempt any registered society from any of the provisions of this ordinance or could direct that such provisions could apply to such society with such modification as could be specified in the order (Cooperative Ordinance, 1932 Section 57). Every registered society could, subject to the approval of the Registrar, make by-laws for any issues as were necessary or desirable for the purpose for which the society was established (Cooperative Ordinance, 1932 Section 58).

Under Cooperative Societies Ordinance, 1932, the Registrar was given the power to register cooperative societies. Hence, in 1933, the first cooperative society in Tanganyika was registered as the Kilimanjaro Native Cooperative Union (KNCU) with its affiliated primary societies which became society members of KNCU. The Cooperative Societies Ordinance of 1932 was used to register different cooperatives such as the Ngoni Matengo Cooperative Union (NGOMAT) in 1936, Bukoba Native Cooperative Union (BNCU) in 1949, the Victoria Federation of Cooperative Unions, and others Cooperatives.

The Cooperative Societies Ordinance, 1932 also reflected the political and economic interests of the colonial government. Firstly, the ordinance disseminated the cooperative institution to the people, on the importance of enlightened membership and rendered advisory services to all registered societies. The cooperative ordinance provided that any 10 or more persons who had reached the of age 18 years could form a cooperative society provided that the society embodies the cooperative principles and the major objective that every society had to observe, which was the promotion of the economic interests of the members. Secondly, the ordinance pointed out the powers of the Registrar of Cooperatives. These powers included the power of approval of any amendment on the by-laws, power to sanction the granting of loans, approval of the investment of the society's funds, approval to distribute bonuses, the power to conduct an inquiry, and inspection and dissolution of a society.

Examining the Cooperative Societies Ordinance, 1932 it is evident that observance of the principles, especially the democratic principle, was limited. The ordinance empowered a registered society to apply to the Governor to compel producers in a given area to sell their produce to the societies. Such compulsion was carried out in Kilimanjaro with the provision of imposition of fines or imprisonment for defaulters. It therefore seems that the ordinance imposed government control on the growth of the cooperative movement (Sekirasa, Z.1. 1992).

The cooperative ordinance amendment in 1952 gave the Registrar the power to dissolve a society's committee, which in his opinion may have been guilty of mismanagement, and to transfer administration of their affairs to members appointed by him. The main reason for the colonial government to do this was that people lacked managerial skills. Sekirasa (1992: 16) challenges this reason arguing that the colonial interest was not to develop a cooperative as a voluntary and democratic institution, but rather as a government agent with the aim of promoting the colonial economy.

8.2 Cooperative Societies Ordinance of 1963

Great cooperative changes occurred after Tanganyika became independent. It was realized by the newly independent government that cooperative activities brought success among the peasants. Due to the fact that agriculture was the back-bone of the economy, the government, under the respective Ministry for Cooperatives passed a new legislation through which cooperative societies could be registered and operated. The Cooperative Societies Ordinance 1963 was enacted and repealed the Cooperative Societies Ordinance, 1932. The minister of cooperatives had the power to register cooperatives even if the Registrar had already refused to do so. The Registrar's decisions were subject to the review by the minister, thus there was high political pressure. The Cooperative Societies Act, 1963 (Tanganyika Government, 1963) waived the economic viability test for cooperatives registration as it was contained in Cooperative Societies Ordinance, 1932. As a result many cooperatives were registered but most of them were weak economically. From 1962 – 1966, 862 cooperative societies were registered (Mbiro, 1992: 39).

8.3 Cooperative Societies Act of 1968

In 1967, the government announced the Arusha Declaration on Socialism and Self Reliance as a guiding policy in development. The government announced that cooperatives were important to social and economic development. This was contained in government paper number 4 of 1967. The paper provided that cooperatives were institutions which would help in building socialism and self-reliance. A new cooperative law which would reflect the political objective contained in the Arusha Declaration was needed land this gave way to the Cooperative Societies Act of 1968 being enacted (United Republic of Tanzania, 1968 (a)).

The Cooperatives Societies Act, 1968 had the main aim of accommodating some new developments brought about by the Arusha Declaration. The Cooperative Societies Act, 1968 repealed and replaced the Cooperative Societies Act, 1963. Cooperatives were expected to accelerate the development of the backward rural sector and the government policy on cooperatives reflected the colonial institutional framework. The government policy was carried out in the following ways: first, establishment of cooperatives in the areas which were lagging behind. Second, promotion of new types of cooperatives, for instance transport, consumer cooperatives, savings and credit cooperatives.

The cooperative movement that was considered ideal for the African setting was a source of conflict and embarrassment to both members and the government over their performance. President Nyerere appointed a Commission of Enquiry in 1966. The commission found the following setbacks (defects) in the cooperative movement:

a) Uninformed membership;

b) Lack of democracy at the union level;

c) Shortage of appropriate manpower; and

d) Absence in the cooperative movement of a corps of skilled people (United Republic of Tanzania (URT) 1966(a) 9-11).

The report of the Commission of Enquiry led to the enactment of the Cooperative Societies, Act 1968. (URT 1968(a)) The new act was not a departure from the Cooperative Societies Ordinance, 1932. Similar to the Cooperative Societies Ordinance 1932, this Cooperative act made the Registrar a referral point of all the societies' power. The Registrar's power over a cooperative society is revealed in the following provisions of the Cooperative Societies Act, 1968.

Section 10 gave the Registrar power to register a cooperative society if he/she were satisfied that such a society was complying with the provisions contained in the act. The Registrar was also given power to sanction any amendment effected to the by-laws by members and to exercise all audit functions pertaining to a cooperative society.

Section 11 gave the Registrar the power to dissolve the committee of a society and appoint one or more suitable persons to manage its affairs. This was a contradiction to the principle of member democratic control that vested control of the affairs of a registered society in a general meeting. The Registrar could also remove the management without consulting the members during a general meeting. Other powers of the Registrar included the power to sanction amalgamation and division of societies, to cancel registration of societies, and to appoint liquidators.

These powers were intended to serve the supervisory role. In the analysis, we see that the powers of the Registrar undermined the principle of self-help and self-determination due to excessive state interference, especially when one recalls that the state had earlier declared that cooperatives were institutions through which the policy of socialism and self-reliance could be implemented. Another legislation enacted during this period was the Unified Cooperative Societies, Act 1968 (URT 1968 (b)). This act established a commission of five members to handle all personnel matters of cooperatives. This was aimed at preventing nepotism and uneven distribution of personnel.

As per section 8 of the Unified Cooperative Societies Act 1968, the commission was entrusted with such functions as to preserve and introduce the terms and conditions of service; appoint persons to hold or act in any office, and to exercise control measures.

The problem of the commission and its interference were due to the fact that it was superimposed on the societies without itself being a part of the movement. This trend of government interference culminated in the abolition of the cooperative unions in 1976.

Prior to the dissolution of cooperative unions and their affiliated societies, a number of factors bore negative impacts on the cooperatives. This was the period when one party rule was consolidated and assumed supreme authority over all matters. From 1973 to 1976, it was a period of intensive villagization, resulting in the uprooting of peasants from their homes and they were sent to new sites to start Ujamaa Villages.

The Cooperative Societies Act, 1968 provided in Section 9 the application procedures for registration of the society to the Registrar. For instance, application for registration had to be accompanied by 3 copies of the by-laws of the society. Section 10 concerned the power of the Registrar to register or to refuse to register societies that had no proper provision made for their financing. Also, if another cooperative society existed within the same locality and engaged in similar activities, a new society could not be registered.

Section 74 called for the compulsory amalgamation of cooperative societies so as to strengthen them economically and socially. Despite this, economically strong cooperative unions like KNCU and BNCU resisted amalgamation with weaker societies as they claimed they could not to benefit from their association. Despite their resistance, government intervened and by 1974 all regions had their own regional cooperative unions.

The Cooperative Societies Act, 1968 gave the government power to intervene, encourage, and supervise the cooperative movement. The government directed villages that reached the highest stage of development to be registered as multipurpose cooperative societies for producing, processing, and marketing farm products (Lyimo, 1983). This strengthened cooperative unions for marketing crops in areas where there was little resistance to the measures, such as in Mtwara, Iringa, Mbeya, and Kigoma. The Act enhanced the expansion of cooperative movements by registering more primary societies and cooperative unions. It also encouraged more primary societies to affiliate with unions for more effective operations in the regions. The legislation also helped to improve agricultural production to some extent by encouraging cooperative societies to provide quality agricultural products.

The Cooperative Societies Act, 1968 stood contrary to democratic cooperative principles since the methods and procedures pursued by the government to solve cooperatives' problems were in the powers of the Registrar to exercise control measures. Act also went against the cooperative principle of political neutrality. This was because the act empowered cooperatives to be instruments for implementing the TANU party's socialist ideology. The minister's political arm in cooperatives which was introduced in the Cooperative Societies Ordinance, 1963 was removed in the Cooperative Societies Act 1968. However, in the 1970s, TANU dominated cooperative activities in that the General Secretary of the Cooperative Union of Tanzania (CUT) was also a member of the National Executive Committee of the ruling political party (TANU). The party exercised its supremacy and directed the government to involve cooperatives more in rural development and in implementing the TANU party's socialist

8.4 Villages and Ujamaa Villages Act No. 21 of 1975

Registering villages as cooperatives using the Cooperatives Societies Act, 1968 was not in line with the national policy of ujamaa which recognized villages as such. TANU party directed the government to pass a bill to recognize and register villages. The act was passed in 1975 and it was called the Villages and Ujamaa Villages Act of 1975 (United Republic of Tanzania, 1975).

Registered Villages were supposed to have not less than 250 households settled in a particular area. The villages would function as if they were multipurpose cooperative societies provided that no other cooperative registered using the Cooperative Societies Act, 1968 was operating there. The villages performed their activities as socialist rural organizations. The ambiguity was that cooperative content was not designed in these ujamaa villages.

The principle of voluntary membership was not applied in village multi-purpose cooperative societies because membership was compulsory. By being a member of a village, one automatically became a member of a rural cooperative organization. There was also no cooperative democratic organization because village decisions were applied as decisions on cooperatives. Following the registration of villages using, the Villages and Ujamaa Villages Act, 1975, the cooperative societies and regional cooperative unions which were registered using Cooperative Societies Act, 1968 were abolished in 1976.

8.5 Cooperative Societies Act of 1982

8.5.1 A New Legislation

After the abolition of marketing cooperatives in 1976, government marketing organizations and crop authorities took over the role of cooperatives. These bodies bought crops directly from villages. This created difficulties as farmers had no place to discuss with these buyers and had no means of communicating with the relevant authorities concerning issues they might have had. For instance, farmers had no way to discuss the prices offered for their produce, which served only to increase their sense of exploitation.

In November 1980, the Prime Minister appointed a twenty-two man committee to collect information about whether to return the cooperative movement or not. The committee recommended re-introduction of cooperatives and stated that they should be registered using the Cooperative Societies Act, 1968 and not the Villages Act of 1975. The government accepted the report and enacted the Cooperative Societies Act, 1982, which provided for restructuring, formation, constitution, registration, and the functioning of cooperative societies. The Cooperative Societies Act, 1982 gave legal basis for establishing new cooperatives (United Republic of Tanzania (URT), 1982). This act repealed and replaced the cooperative societies Act 1968 and replaced the Village Act 1975 which was repealed by section 1951(c) of local government (District Authority), 1982. The Cooperative Societies Act, 1982 Section 4 defined a cooperative society as an association of people who have joined together with an objective of promoting the economic and social welfare of its members. The society was to be operated democratically on the basis of the principles, methods and procedures of cooperation.

Cooperative Societies Act, 1982 Section 24 described the criteria for membership in a rural cooperative society. Every person who had attained the age of eighteen years and who was a resident of the village, in occupation of land, possessed a special skill relevant to a trade, or was following an occupation relevant to the rural society's objectives within its area of operation as defined in its by-laws should be a member of the rural cooperative society of the village in which he/she was a resident. Three years later the controversial provision was amended to every person who was a resident of a village could a member of a rural cooperative society. This amendment was in accordance with the principle of voluntary membership in cooperatives.

8.5.2 *Objectives of the Cooperative Societies*

The objectives of cooperative societies which were stated in Cooperative societies Act, 1982:

a) To accelerate the building of socialism by bringing about socialist development both in rural and urban areas;

b) To foster the development of cooperative farming in rural areas as a means of modernizing and developing agriculture and of eliminating exploitation in rural areas;

c) To satisfy the cultural needs of members as well as to increase their social and political awareness;

d) To improve the material living conditions of its members; and

e) To promote Cooperative education amongst its members (Cooperative Societies Act, 1982 Section 4).

Part V of the Cooperative Societies Act 1982 provided for the formation and organization of cooperative societies. Section 14 provided for the structure of cooperative societies which included primary societies, secondary societies, and apex organization. Section 15 provided for the formation of primary societies. Ten or more people could form a primary cooperative society in a village and it had to be economically viable.

The Cooperative Societies Act, 1982 Section 15(3) provided for the formation of a cooperative union at regional level on the condition that it had to be economically viable. A cooperative union could also be formed at the district level but an approval of a minister was necessary. Section 16 of the cooperative Act, 1982 stipulated that primary societies could form secondary societies and secondary societies could form an apex organization which was a cooperative at national level.

8.5.3 *Levels of Cooperatives*

a) Primary Societies

The Cooperative Societies Act, 1982 recognized the rural primary cooperatives as multipurpose cooperative societies which could undertake all kinds of business operations as provided under section 22 of this act. By contrast, in urban areas there were single-purpose cooperatives. Once a cooperative society was registered in a rural area, no other type of cooperative was allowed to operate within the same area of operation. In villages, villagers were supposed to organize themselves into cooperative groups so that they could pursue trade and within that, they could work under the rural cooperative societies. The rural cooperative societies had the following functions:

(i) To prepare the economic plan of the society in consultation with the village council;

(ii) To purchase, preserve and distribute agricultural inputs and other resources for use in the economic activities of the society;

(iii) To provide, operate, and maintain machinery for the processing of agricultural products;

(iv) To seek and employ the best methods of agricultural production so as to ensure an improved yield of agricultural products in rural areas;

(v) To provide, operate, and maintain farm equipment including machinery for use by or on behalf of the members in the production of agricultural products;

(vi) To collect agricultural products from their members and to deliver those products for sale;

(vii) To coordinate all economic activities of the villages; and

(viii) To establish, operate, and maintain large scale farms for agricultural production (Cooperative Societies Act, 1982 Section 29).

b) The Cooperative Unions

As secondary organizations, the unions operated at district and regional levels depending on economic viability and the wishes of the people. The laws discouraged the formation of specialized secondary organizations for other types of cooperatives, such as housing cooperatives, by empowering the Registrar to issue directives which would make it compulsory for other types of primary societies in the area to join the union. The objectives of secondary societies were to facilitate the operations of primary societies. The main functions of the cooperative unions were:

(i) To collect produce from primary societies and to process and deliver agricultural products for marketing;

(ii) To procure and distribute agricultural inputs required by member primary societies;

(iii) To provide finance for the purchase of agricultural products from their member primary societies;

(iv) To manage, supervise and coordinate the activities of other societies providing special production services to agriculturalists;

(v) To acquire, maintain and operate building equipment for the assembling, warehousing, and transportation of agricultural products belonging to member primary cooperative societies;

(vi) To establish, operate, and maintain large-scale farms;

(vii) To establish and operate a cooperative savings and credit services for member societies; and

(viii) To provide accounting and audit services to member societies (Cooperative Societies Act, 1982 Section 18).

c) The Cooperative at the National Level

This was implemented at the national level and was formed by district and regional cooperative unions. It represented both ideological as well as business interests of the movement and it was required to undertake income-generating activities for its survival. The apex organization had the following functions:

(i) To coordinate the economic plans of the member societies and forward them to the ministry for incorporation in the national plan;

(ii) To render services designed to ensure efficiency and uniformity in the conduct of the business of its member societies, such as standardizing their book-keeping, accounting and other procedures for auditing services and providing audit services to those societies;

(iii) To formulate, maintain, and regulate the terms and conditions of services of persons employed in the apex organization and secondary societies;

(iv) To carry on to encourage and assist educational and advisory work relating to cooperative enterprises and disseminate information on cooperative principles and practices;

(v) To reduce operating costs by arranging for group bonding of cooperative society employees and by making bulk purchases of book-keeping stationery and other supplies for sale to its members;

(vi) To provide consultative services to member societies;

(vii) To represent member societies in collective bargaining;

(viii) To print, publish, and circulate newspapers or other publications designed to foster or increase interest in cooperative enterprises, principles and practices; and

(ix) To represent its member societies in international conferences (Cooperative Societies Act, 1982, Section 20).

Part VII of the Act provided for the rights and liabilities of members. For instance, section 78 provided that every member of a registered society had only one vote in the affairs of society and was entitled to attend the general meeting of the society and to record his vote in regard to any matter of decision making of such a meeting.

There are other provisions such as responsibilities of the minister (Part III), appointment of the Registrar and his functions (Part IV), registration of societies (Part VI), duties of registered societies (Part VIII), management of registered societies (Part X), inspection of the society's affairs (Part XII), and others.

The Registrar was empowered to amalgamate any two or more societies as one and divide any society respectively. Section 138 (1) provided that where the Registrar was satisfied that it was in the interests of two or more registered societies to amalgamate as a single society and that such amalgamation would not be against the public interests, he/she could, by notice in writing, require the societies to amalgamate. Section 140(1) pertained to the division of a society. Where the Registrar was satisfied that it was in the interest of an existing registered society to divide itself into two or more new registered societies and that such division would not be against the public interest, he may, by notice in writing, require the existing society to so divide itself.

Section 86 provided for a registered society to amend its by-laws. Such amendment would be valid after it had been registered under this act. If the Registrar was satisfied that the amendment of the by-laws was not contrary to the act, he/she should register the amendment.

Cooperative Societies Act, 1982 Sections 106 (1) empowered the Registrar to dissolve elected committee members of a society and to appoint a fit and proper person or persons to carry out the functions of the committee. Section 114 empowered the Registrar to direct societies as to where to deposit their funds, and to conduct enquiries and inspections into the constitutional and financial affairs and activities and gather any information necessary to that effect.

Sekirasa (1992) noted that the situation was further aggravated as the cooperative movement was one of the CCM party's mass organizations. CCM continued to appoint the Secretary General of the cooperative mass organization (CUT). The democratic principle of a cooperative was therefore violated.

8.6 The Cooperative Societies Act of 1991

A new cooperative societies' act was passed by parliament in April 1991 as a tool of appropriate for strengthening the cooperative movement. Sekirasa (1991: 35) argued that in a government policy statement on the state of cooperatives, the government acknowledged that cooperatives were experiencing numerous problems which included non-involvement of the cooperators on matters which affected them, government intervention into the affairs of the cooperative, ineffective financial systems and undemocratic managerial practices.

The Cooperative Societies Act, 1991 incorporated amendments which had been made in the cooperative Societies, Act 1982 in Sections 15 and 24 to make membership of cooperative societies voluntary and to provide for the registration of productive cooperatives within the village boundaries.

The Cooperative Societies Act, 1991 incorporated the amendments of the 1982 Act, was amended in sections 2,13,14, and 16 to allow the establishment and registration of a National Apex Organization for the whole of Tanzania. The Cooperative Societies Act 1991 also incorporated the amendment of cooperative Act. Sections 15, 22, 23, 24, 29 and 76 to enable the formation of cooperative societies based on common bonds and for the interest of the cooperators themselves, guided by the quest for economic viability but without being compelled to conduct other business as well, and without administrative limitations. Members of the cooperative societies were also to be identified by acquiring shares and by paying entry fees. These changes were necessary and basic to implementing the goals of the cooperative spirit.

Under the Cooperative Societies Act, 1991, members of the primary cooperative who had a common bond such as cooperatives for industrial production, housing, construction, animal husbandry, growing of coffee, cashew nuts, cotton, and others, were at liberty to set up their cooperative s union. Cooperative unions which performed similar activities were in turn free to create their own Apex organization which could then set up their respective National Federation. This national body would represent the cooperatives within and outside the country, and would also cater to the education and economic needs of the members.

Under the Cooperative Societies Act, 1991, a cooperative society was defined as an association of persons who voluntarily joined together for the purpose of achieving a common need through the formulation of a democratically controlled organization and who made equitable contribution to the capital required for formation of such an organization and who accepted the risks and reaped the benefits of the undertaking in which they actively participated.

The new cooperative law was distinguished by two significant departures from the Cooperative law of 1982, namely: The words *socialist outlook* were deleted from the objective clause regarding building socialism by bringing about socialist development. Secondly, the clause in section 4(b) of the 1982 Act is not present in the 1991 legislation. The clause reads, in part, to foster the development of cooperatives farming in rural areas, and modernizing agriculture as a means of eliminating exploitation in the rural areas. Sekirasa (1992) asked whether the omission of socialism and socialist development implies that cooperatives would no longer be a tool for the implementation of political goals. Whereas in section 5 of the 1982 Act reads that the state shall protect the cooperative societies by support, guidance, and supervision, the 1991 Act Section 5 states that state shall protect cooperatives by offering support, guidance, and advice. It should be noted that the word *supervising* was replaced by the word *advice*. This shows that the government had learned some lessons.

Part II of the Cooperatives Societies Act, 1991 stipulated objectives of cooperatives and the protection of the cooperative movement. This part defined cooperative society as an association of persons who have voluntarily joined together with the objective of promoting the economic and social welfare of its members. In accordance with cooperative principles, cooperative societies should strive to improve the material living conditions of members, to satisfy the cultural needs of members as well as increase their social and political awareness, and to promote cooperative education among them. This part also stipulated the protection of cooperatives. It provided that the state should protect cooperatives by offering support, guidance, and advice.

Parts III and IV highlighted the roles and functions of the Minister and the Registrar. Such power intimately worked against the democratic control of the cooperatives. In the new law the words to exercise control over cooperatives are omitted and instead the words the Registrar promotes, inspects, and advice cooperative societies are used. This did not reflect the diminished role of the Registrar. It was still patently obvious that the Registrar continued to yield power in sensitive matters. Other provisions undermined the principles and are discussed below:

Firstly, cooperative organizations should actively cooperate at local, national, and international levels. Despite this cooperative principle, the government did not want to lose power over cooperatives. Secondly, the principle of democratic control was affected by Section 66, which vested in the Registrar the mandate to assess performance of any management committee and to advise the general meeting on whether to suspend or dissolve any committee of a society. Although the special general meeting could differ with the Registrar, the members were threatened by Cooperative Societies Act, 1991, Section 66(2) which stated that, "where the special general meeting resolves to disagree with the advice of the Registrar on financial malpractices the effects of which the society is rendered unable to settle its liabilities, the members shall be liable for the payment of the debts." Again the Registrar's role showed that the government was not ready to keep its hands away from cooperatives. Under Cooperative Societies Act, 1991 Section 70(3), it was stated that a society should not issue bonds or debentures without the authority of the Registrar.

Further, in Section 71(1), consent of the Registrar was mandatory for normal business credited to bona fide persons to whom goods have been sold and again, except with the permission of the registrar, a society could not lend money on the security of any movable property. The Registrar could by a general or special order, prohibit or restrict the lending of money by any society on the security of immovable property. This was unnecessary interference in managing financial resources of the societies. The Cooperative Act 1991 was intended to strengthen the achievements of the Cooperative Societies Act 1982 and continued to emphasize objectives of cooperatives societies. The Act of 1991 had many provisions for cooperatives not much different from those of the 1982 Act. Voluntary amalgamation and division of societies was allowed. Section 97(1) stated that any two or more societies could amalgamate as a single society when two thirds of members of societies were present at the time and place of the voting meeting. Subsection two (2) provided the conditions which would oblige the Registrar to register an amalgamated society: if two or more registered societies resolved to amalgamate as a single society and the proposed by-laws of the amalgamated societies were unobjectionable; and if the proposed amalgamation was not against the members' and public's interests.

Section 99 provided for societies wishing to divide were required to have a resolution that contained proposals for division of assets and liabilities of the existing society among the proposed new societies. Section 99 (3) provided that the registrar could advise on voluntary division if the existing society had resolved to divide itself into two or more new societies. The proposed new societies had to be economically viable, and division only possible when not against the interest of the members or that of the public.

A number of problems posed obstacles to the successful achievement of the Act's aims and objectives. The bottom-up approach had become a difficulty strategy to be implemented successfully as farmers had been living under the support of the government, and hence there was a sense of dependence which critically eroded peasants' confidence. There was lack of appropriate knowledge and the peasants believed that it was the role of the government to initiate the formation of the cooperatives and to provide them with necessary financial resources, to supervise and control them in achieving the goals set by policy makers.

8.7 The Cooperative Societies Act No. 20 of 2003

The Cooperative Societies Act, 2003 was intended to make better provisions for the formation, constitution, registration, and operation of cooperative societies, and for other matters incidental to or otherwise with those purposes.

8.7.1 *Objects of Cooperatives Societies*

Part II of the Cooperative Societies Act, 2003 stated that a cooperative is society which has as its objectives the promotion of the economic and social interests of its members by means of a common undertaking based upon mutual aid and which conforms to the cooperative principles or as a society which is established for the purpose of facilitating operations of societies could be registered as a cooperative society under the Cooperative Societies Act 2003 with or without limited liability (Cooperative Societies Act, 2003 Section 4(1).

Cooperative principles and methods used in the operation and administration of a cooperative society should be:

a) A voluntary organization, open to all persons able to use their services and willing to accept the responsibilities of membership, without gender, social, political, or religious discrimination;

b) Democratic organizations controlled by members who actively participate in setting their policies and making decisions, both men and women, serving as elected representatives and accountable to the membership. In primary cooperatives, members have equal voting rights, and cooperatives at other levels are also organized in a democratic manner;

c) Members contribute equitably, and democratically control the capital of the cooperative;

d) Autonomous self-help organizations controlled by their members, if they enter into agreement with other organizations, including governments, or raise capital from external sources, they do so on terms that ensure democratic control by their members and maintain their cooperative autonomy;

e) The organization provides education and training for their members, elected representatives, managers, and employees so they can contribute effectively in the development of their cooperatives;

f) Organizations inform general public, particularly young people and opinion leaders, about the nature and benefits of cooperation;

g) Organizations serve their members most effectively and strengthen the cooperative movement by working through local, national, and international structures; and

h) Organizations work for the sustainable development of their communities through policies approved by their members (Cooperative Societies Act, 2003 Section 4(2)).

Cooperative Societies Act, 2003 Part III provides for the appointment of the Registrar of Cooperatives, Deputy Registrar and Assistant Registrars. The President of Tanzania appoints a public officer to be the Registrar of Cooperative Societies. The functions of the Registrar are stated in Section 11 (1).

a) To register, promote, inspect, and advise cooperative societies in accordance with the provisions of the Cooperative Societies Act, 2003;

b) To advise the Minister on any matter relating to cooperative societies and in particular in respect of any assistance financial or otherwise, which may be required by cooperative societies;

c) To encourage the establishment of cooperative societies in all sectors of the economy and to assist cooperative societies to increase their efficiency;

d) To provide services designed to assist in the formation, organization, and operation of societies and to give advice on cooperative management to all kinds of societies registered under the Cooperative Societies Act. 2003;

e) To perform such other functions in relation to the development and well being of cooperative societies such as may be directed by the Minister; and

f) To promote or facilitate the education and training of members and staff of cooperative societies.

The President of Tanzania appoints a Deputy Registrar from among public officers. The Deputy Registrar performs such functions and duties as may be directed by the Registrar or as may be required under the Cooperative Societies Act. Upon due authorization, the Deputy Registrar exercises any of the functions of the Registrar. Assistant Registrars are appointed by the Minister of Cooperatives amongst Principal cooperative officers to assist the Registrar in carrying out his/her duties and function under the Cooperative Societies Act (Cooperative Societies Act, 2003 Section 12).

Registration of cooperative societies is provided for in Part V of the Act. Applications for registration shall be made to the registrar in the prescribed form accompanied by four copies of proposed by-laws of the society signed by the applicant, a report of a feasibility study or project write-up indicating the liability of the society and such other information in respect with the society as the Registrar may require (Cooperative Societies Act, 2003 Section 24).

The members of the Board shall be elected by the general meeting of the society and shall hold office for a period of up to 9 years (Section 63(2)). Restrictions relating to members of the Board of a registered society hence no member shall hold office on profit under the society section 65(1). No member shall be elected as a Board member if he owns, controls or influences business like that of the cooperative society (Section 65(5)) Where the special general meeting resolves to suspend members of the board it shall elect a care taker board from amongst the delegates to administer the affairs of the society and require the suspended members to state their objection in writings in the next general meeting. (Cooperative Societies Act, 2003 Section 66).

Part X of the Cooperative Societies Act, 2003 included revenue of registered societies and any money derived from fees or charges are specified by the by-laws of the society (Section 69 (1)). Management of the revenue and funds of registered societies is controlled by the by-laws of the society. Restriction on loans prohibits a registered society from granting a loan to a non-member (Section 71(1). A registered society may invest its funds in interest bearing deposit in financial institutions. Investment of funds on shares of any other registered society, government bonds, and other securities or in such other investments as the Registrar may by order, with approval of the Minister, of Cooperatives declare to be authorized investment (Cooperative Societies Act, 2003 Section 73).

Dissolution of societies is provided for in Part XIV. The act provides for appeal against cancellation of registration. Where the registration of a society is cancelled under the provisions of Section 97 or 98 of the act, any member of the society, from which the registration is cancelled, may within thirty days from the date of the order canceling the registration, appeal against such an order to the minister (Cooperative Act, 2003 Section, 99).

The Act also provides for the power of the Registrar to assess damages against delinquent promoters (Section 107). Part XV considers offences. Section 121 points out procedures on the penalty for soliciting violation of contracts. Any person, firm, or company having knowledge or notice of a registered society which has as one of its objectives the disposal of any articles as part of its business, who solicits or persuades any person to sell or deliver in violation of the by-laws of that society is liable to a fine. Cooperative Societies Acts, 1982, and 2003 conferred wide powers on the Registrar. These include: registering a society, dissolving societies, directing inquiry, inspection, and voluntary amalgamation of societies. Cooperative acts have been changing to respond to the changing socio-economic and political situations. Acts are changing to make better provision for the formation, constitution, registration, and operation of cooperative societies.

Conclusion

The various forms cooperatives acquired responded to the material conditions prevailing in the country at a particular time. Problems which cooperatives have gone through show that the only way for cooperatives to thrive in this country is to allow them to operate on the basics of principles of cooperatives, Sekirasa (1992: 49) emphasized that so long as principles of cooperation are not adhered to, and so long as the government continues to dominate cooperative societies, the future of member controlled cooperatives in Tanzania is uncertain. Since 1932, there have been new, revised and amended cooperative laws in response to social and economic developments. The role of cooperatives legislations has been to establish and strengthen the Cooperative. The Cooperative Societies Act, 2003 succeeded to increase the number and the quality of cooperative societies within the country. By June 2008, there were 2614 agricultural marketing cooperative societies, 4780 savings and credits cooperative societies, 71 livestock cooperative societies, 129 fishing cooperative societies, 11 housing cooperative societies, 3 mining cooperative societies, 185 industrial cooperative societies, 98 water irrigation cooperative societies, 4 transport cooperative societies, 103 consumer cooperative societies, and 553 service and other cooperative societies. In total, by June 2008, there were 8,551 Primary Cooperative Societies (S. Maghimbi, 2008).

References

Cliffe, L. and G. Cunningham, 'Ideology, Organization and the Settlement Experiences in Tanzania in Cliffe, L. and J.S. Saul (eds.), 1973, 'Socialism in Tanzania' in *An Interdisciplinary Reader* Vol.2, Dar es Salaam: East African Publishing House, pp. 131 – 140.

Kihwelo, P.F., 1998, State control over cooperatives in Tanzania; A critique to Comparative Societies amendment Act 1997, L.L.M. Dissertation presented to the Faculty of Law, University of Dar es Salaam.

Kimario, M., 1992, *Marketing Cooperatives in Tanzania; Problems and Prospects,* Dar es Salaam: Dar es Salaam University Press.

Lyimo F.F., 1975, Problems and Prospects of Ujamaa Development in Moshi District, M.A. Dissertation presented to the University of Dar es Salaam.

Lyimo F.F, 1983, Peasant Production and Cooperative Experiences in Tanzania: Case studies of villages in Moshi (rural), and Urambo Districts, Ph.D. Dissertation, University of Wisconsin-Madison.

Maghimbi, S., 2008, Consultancy Research Report on Cooperatives in Tanzania Mainland, Dar es Salaam: Unpublished.

Mally Wilson J.A., 1974, Peasant production experiences in Tanzania, L.L.M. Dissertation presented to the Faculty of Law University of Dar es Salaam.

Mbiro, Vinton Willgis, 1992, State Control Over Cooperative Law in Tanzania (Mainland): An Appraisal of Some New Developments on Cooperative Laws, L.L.M. Dissertation presented to the Faculty of Law, University of Dar es Salaam.

Minde, E.M., 1982, The changing nature of cooperatives in Tanzania, L.L.M. Dissertation presented to the Faculty of Law, University of Dar es Salaam.

Nyerere J.K., 1968, *Freedom and socialism,* Dar es Salaam: Oxford University Press.

Sekirasa, Z.I., 1992, A comparative study of the 1982 and 1991 Cooperative Acts in light of the cooperative principles, L.L.M. Dissertation presented to the Faculty of Law, University of Dar es Salaam.

Tanganyika government, 1963, *Cooperative Societies. Chapter 211 of the Laws (Revised) (Principal Legislation),* Dar es Salaam: Government Printer.

Tanganyika Government, 1932, 'The Cooperative Ordinance of Tanganyika, 1932', also published in Strickland, C. F., 1933, *Cooperation for Africa,* London: Oxford University Press, pp. 98-119.

United Republic of Tanzania, 1977, *Interm Constitution of Tanzania,* Dar es Salaam: Government Printer.

United Republic of Tanzania, 1991, *Cooperative Societies Act, 1991,* Dar es Salaam: Government Printer.

United Republic of Tanzania (URT), 1982, *Cooperative Societies Act, 1982,* Dar es Salaam: Government Printer.

United Republic of Tanzania (URT), 2005, The *Cooperative Societies Act, 2003* Revised Education, 2004, Dar es Salaam: Government Printer.

United Republic of Tanzania (URT), 1968(a), *Cooperative Societies Act, 1968,* Dar es Salaam: Government Printer.

United Republic of Tanzania (URT), 1968(b), *Unified Cooperative Societies Act 1968,* Dar es Salaam: Government Printer.

United Republic of Tanzania, 1975, The Villages and Ujamaa Villages *(Registration, Designation and Administration)* Act, 1975, Dar es Salaam: Government Printer.

9

Types of Cooperatives

There are many criteria which are used in classifying cooperatives. These criteria include work performed by cooperatives, groups of members served by cooperatives, and levels of operation of cooperatives. There is no short way of classifying them because one cooperative may belong to more than one classification. For example, a cooperative may belong to production, marketing, and processing and at the same time operate as a primary Cooperative Society or a cooperative Union.

Various cooperatives are found in different countries. The major types of cooperatives include agricultural, industrial, consumers, savings and credit cooperatives. Ngeze, P.B. (1975: 30-39) identified three major types of cooperatives in Tanzania: the marketing cooperatives, producers' cooperatives, and savings and credit cooperatives. Under these three types, there are other small types such as livestock and milk cooperatives in agriculture, and marketing cooperatives. The forces which motivate people to organize a cooperative can also determine its type.

9.1 Classification of Cooperatives According to Work Performed

Cooperatives are grouped according to the work they perform for their members. Workers may organize cooperatives to pursue any of a large number of occupational interests in industrial business ventures, or to produce and market products, or to provide any of the many services used in everyday living.

Workers' cooperatives are unique both as cooperatives and businesses. Workers participate directly in decisions that affect them in their workplace as well as those that determine the growth and success of the business. They provide members with employment along with the ownership and control of the enterprises and in return receive a fair share of the profits and control over the way their work is organized, performed, and managed.

Workers' Cooperatives apply distinctive worker cooperative principles which specify that worker members:

a) Take the full risks and benefits of working, owning, and operating their cooperative business;

b) Equitably contribute to and benefit from the capital of their cooperative;

c) Decide how the net income, or the net loss, is allocated; and

d) Govern and control the enterprise on a one-member, one-vote basis.

In Tanzania, workers' cooperative societies include the following:

9.1.1 Cooperatives for Harvesting Natural Products

Timber and logs marketing cooperatives started in recent years in Tanzania. Members of these cooperatives have the responsibility of harvesting timber and logs and selling them as a cooperative enterprise.

Bee Keeping Cooperatives deal with keeping bees and collecting honey and wax. Every member keeps bees and harvests honey and wax which are then stored by the cooperative, put in packages, and then sold on behalf of the members.

9.1.2 Cooperatives for Arts and Craft

A wood carving and art works cooperative was established in July 1961 in Mtwara. Wood carving and art works cooperatives have also been established in other regions. The cooperatives sell their products to domestic and foreign buyers. Cooperatives for art works produce and sell products like baskets, pots, handbags, ropes, and other traditional goods.

9.1.3 Fisheries Cooperatives

Fishing cooperatives are found in areas near lakes, big rivers, and the ocean and they deal with fishing activities. Members buy fishing equipment like dhows, canoes and nets. They catch fish together and divide the catch or sell it together. Fishermen form cooperatives to access technical and education services for pursuing their business. (Ngeze, P. B.1975: 34).

9.1.4 Mining Cooperatives

Mining cooperatives have been established in Tanzania. Members of these cooperatives are diggers of minerals including gold, tanzanite, and other minerals. Members of cooperatives work or dig together and sell through the cooperative whatever quantity of minerals they find and divide the profits.

9.2 Classification of Cooperatives According to Groups Served

Cooperatives serve many groups of people. Cooperatives serve farmers, consumers, workers and other groups in varied occupations. The main types of cooperatives that serve groups of people are analyzed in this section.

9.2.1 Farmers' Cooperatives

Farmers Cooperatives are the oldest and most important type of cooperative in Tanzania. They are member-owned and controlled cooperatives. Farmers' cooperatives help producers to assure markets and achieve economies of scale and gain market power through joint marketing, bargaining, processing, and purchasing of supplies and services. Farmers' Cooperatives have subtypes.

a) Cooperative Farming Societies

Under this type of farming the members of society cultivate farms collectively and sell farm products through their cooperative society. Cooperative farming societies aim at increasing agricultural productivity, improving farming efficiency, improving the quality of produce and raising the standard of living of farmers (Cliffe, et al. 1975). Cooperative farming benefits members in the following ways:

(i) Cooperative farming maximizes agricultural production so that it results in a large gain to members. Cooperative farming facilitates bulk buying and selling. The cooperative farming society purchases farm inputs in bulk in order to pay lower prices. A cooperative society has better borrowing power than individual peasants. The peasants find it tough to secure loans when they approach financial institutions as individuals. A cooperative society enables its members to reap the benefits of large-scale farming; and

(ii) A cooperative farming society should be a voluntary organization and with no scope for coercing persons into becoming members.

Nevertheless the farming cooperative has many practical difficulties:

- Under cooperative farming the effort is common so people do not take any initiative to work hard as a result there may be a decline in total production;
- When all persons are not equally informed, some people can use the situation to their own advantage. A few brainy members can start exploiting a large number of ignorant and innocent farmers, which leads to deterioration in the living condition of the latter;
- Cooperative farming can create the problem of unemployment due to the use of modern machinery for cultivation of land; and
- Withdrawal of membership can be disastrous for the society. The society works properly only when its members are loyal to it. The farming society suffers when it is not run by honest and efficient management personnel.

b) Farmers' Marketing Cooperatives

With the development of cash crop production, conditions have been favorable for cooperation in the marketing of farm produce. This has become possible because the subsistence economy has gradually been replaced by the commodity type of economy.

Farm products marketing cooperatives in Tanzania have a significant role. The earliest cooperatives were started by cash crop farmers who wanted to avoid exploitation by Asian middlemen. Farmers marketing cooperatives are mainly concerned with assembling, packaging, processing, and selling farm products in both domestic and foreign markets. Cooperatives purchase crops from farmers, then bargain with buyers for prices and conditions of sale. Marketing cooperatives pool the products according to market preferences.

The Farm Products Marketing Society is an organization through which the farmer is guaranteed of a fair return on produce. Marketing constitutes the final stage of the production process through which the farmers earn the rewards for their work. In Tanzania, marketing cooperatives started by marketing cash crops such as coffee and cotton, and later added grains such as rice and maize. They serve their member patrons by purchasing products outright or by functioning on a commission basis and they can bargain with buyers for prices and conditions of selling.

The farm products marketing cooperatives work with these general objectives:

- To fetch the best possible market prices for their members' products;
- To reduce the cost of marketing including costs of transportation, storage and package etc; and
- To compete with the monopolistic power of the private traders (middlemen) who exploit farmers by offering lower prices for their products, manipulate weights and measures, and make unjust assessment of the quality of the products.

There are factors which favor setting up cooperative marketing societies:

- If the place of production is away from the market place, then farmers think of cooperating under the banner of a marketing cooperative society to get the benefits of large-scale transportation and marketing;
- The need for marketing cooperatives arises when the crops grown for marketing in an area need organization of marketing cooperative to sell the agricultural produce;

- Frequent fluctuation in demand necessitates the setting up of the marketing cooperatives to handle products and sell them when demand goes up;
- Marketing cooperatives arrange for the transportation of the farmers' produce which may result in reducing the cost and raising the returns for farmers;
- Marketing cooperative societies make advance payments to farmers with a view to preventing distress sales of produce soon after the harvest; they can wait till they get better prices;
- The pooling and grading of crops is also undertaken by cooperative marketing societies, which have their own warehouses in which the agricultural produce of farmers is stored; and
- As a result of the grading and standardization of goods by marketing cooperatives, consumers may also benefit because they get better quality goods at prices which are lower than those offered by private merchants.

c) Production Supply Cooperatives

The third type of agricultural cooperatives is production supply cooperatives. These cooperatives purchase products and services for their members. They make large scale purchases of seeds, fertilizers, and crop protectants (ie. insecticide, pesticides) and farm equipment and sell them at cost-savings to members.

d) Farmers' Multi-purpose Cooperatives in Villages.

Another variety of farmers' cooperatives in Tanzania were the multi-purpose Cooperatives. The villages functioned as multi-purpose cooperatives registered under the Villages and Ujamaa Villages Act, 1975. The movement of cooperatives towards Ujamaa was achieved, through the formation of production based on multipurpose cooperative in Ujamaa villages. Ujamaa villages had to provide the basis for mobilizing the peasants in a more meaningful way and consequently involve them more actively in their organizations and enable them to defend themselves against exploitation by private marketing organizations. Ujamaa Policy was expected to make cooperatives play an increasingly active role in facilitating the transition of Ujamaa itself (Cliffe, L. et al, 1975). The Ujamaa villages functioning as multi-purpose cooperatives had a role to play in fighting poverty by involving the peasants in cooperative production which would ensure them increased production and more income.

9.2.2 *Savings and Credit Cooperative Societies (SACCOS)*

Savings and Credit Cooperatives promote thrift among members. In Tanzania, savings and credit cooperatives give credit to people to finance activities such as housing construction, land development and small business. Savings and Credit Cooperatives exert a noticeable effect on the development of commodity relations.

In Tanzania, the first African Savings and Credit Cooperative was established in Dar es Salaam in October 1961 called Kianga Credit Cooperative. It aimed to provide a safe place to keep the members' money and to provide credit with soft conditions and a controlled interest rate to its members (Ngeze, P.B (1975: 34-35)). SACCOS are common to many people in Tanzania and they are registered for the promotion of thrift among the members and to create financial support for improving people's wellbeing.

The Savings and Credit Societies (SACCOS) have been expanding fast and in 2008 there were 4780 registered SACCOS in Tanzania ranging from community-based initiatives recruiting community SACCOS members, to workplace-based SACCOS. For instance, the Post and Telecommunication SACCOS is the largest cooperative in Tanzania and it provides savings and credit services to employees of Tanzania Telecommunication Company, Tanzania Postal Bank, and the Communication Regulation Authority (Maghimbi, S. 2009). Savings and Credit Cooperatives are seen as one of the means of achieving a radical transformation of existing social conditions and as a means of reducing poverty (Maslennikov, 1990: 77).

9.2.3 *Consumer Cooperatives*

Consumer Cooperatives Societies are business organizations owned by the customer members. A consumer cooperative may be registered to sell consumer goods and can embark on purchasing, processing and manufacturing of different products. Its prime aim is to increase members' purchasing power and improve people's lives. Consumer cooperatives play a significant role in the economic and social transformation of developing countries. (Maslennikov, 1990: 93). The numbers of consumer cooperatives have tended to grow in developing countries because of the following reasons: Firstly, cooperative trade makes it easier to supply consumers with the necessary goods. Secondly, cooperatives are non-profit organizations so they purchase goods in substantial amounts and sell them on a non-profit basis. Thirdly, cooperatives help maintain stable prices; they do not try to raise prices because many consumers are their shareholders. (Maslennikov, 1990: 95).

Consumer cooperatives in Tanzania were established as an expansion of cooperative services. Members hope to benefit from consumer cooperatives through favorable prices, high quality products and reliable services. Consumer cooperatives are primarily concerned with wholesale and retail trades. They are expected to offer better services to their members and also to provide dividend returns, if any, when the society has made reasonable profit during its year of operation. The broader objective of consumer cooperative societies is to eliminate the dishonest intermediaries in trade whose actions benefit neither the producers nor the consumers. In 2008, there were 103 consumer cooperative societies in Tanzania. The significance and role of consumer cooperatives in Tanzania is expected to grow constantly since their activities are seeking to satisfy the needs of the consumers. Lenin emphasized that, "There must be support and development of Consumers' Cooperative Societies, for they will ensure the swift, regular, and low-cost distribution of products" (Lenin, 1977: 370).

9.2.4 Housing Cooperatives

Housing cooperatives fulfill important social and economic functions. Their existence is associated with rapid population growth and large scale rural migration to towns. Housing cooperatives were first established in Tanzania in the 1970's and aimed at delivering good shelter to the people, The first initiative was a donor-driven joint initiative by the International Cooperative Housing to create a cooperative housing movement in Tanzania. Housing cooperatives organize the construction of housing, which is cooperative property to be rented.

9.3 Classification of Cooperatives According Levels of Operation

Cooperatives are also classified by the levels they serve. Four types of cooperatives are identified this way – local, regional, national, and federal levels. The basis of this classification often reflects a mixture of the size of business operations and the functions that cooperatives perform.

9.3.1 Local Cooperatives

The Local Cooperatives operate from trading centres and they accept individual people who apply for membership and who qualify for membership as defined in the Cooperative Societies Act and by-laws of the societies.

9.3.2 Regional Cooperative Unions

In Tanzania, regional cooperative unions were abolished in 1976 and were again re-established in 1982. Cooperatives which operate at regional administrative levels in Tanzania include Morogoro Regional Cooperative

Union (MORECU), Tanga Regional Cooperative Union (TARECU), Shinyanga Regional Cooperative Union (SHIRECU), to mention but a few. They can also operate at district level like the Cooperative union which operates in Same-Pare district within Kilimanjaro Region, unlike Kilimanjaro Native Cooperative Union (KNCU), which operates in the whole region except the Same - Pare district. The Regional Cooperative Unions play a vital role since they provide manufacturing services which local cooperatives cannot provide due to limited resources. Unions sell goods and services through primary cooperatives. Cooperative Unions collect products from primary societies to Union warehouses and sell the products in the market.

9.3.3 National Cooperative Union

In Tanzania this is the apex organization which was formed and registered to provide, organize and supervise effective centralized services for the member unions and offer cooperative education and training and such other services which are necessary or expedient for its members.

The Apex Cooperative Organization has regional cooperative unions as its members. The Cooperative Union of Tanzania (CUT) was formed in 1961 as an apex cooperative union which had the following responsibilities:

a) To represent the cooperative movement at both national and international levels;

b) To collect and disseminate cooperative information and statistical data;

c) To promote different types of cooperatives;

d) To carry out cooperative education either through its affiliated members or its own educational structures;

e) To carry out publicity work on behalf of the movement;

f) To advise its members on all matters pertaining to cooperative development;

g) To arrange for such audit and supervision of members societies as may be authorized by the Registrar; and

h) To provide assistance to member cooperatives in legal matters. (CUT. 1961: 2).

9.3.4 Federation of Cooperatives

A federation of cooperatives is formed by two or more cooperative unions. While the type of business varies according to the type of member cooperatives, these federations carry out activities such as joint advertising, joint purchasing, and information collection and dissemination from which greater merits are expected to accrue than if they were carried out independently by individual cooperatives.

9.4 Factors which Influence Types of Cooperatives Established

9.4.1 Services needed

There should be a need for a cooperative so that members can get services or goods. For example, need for cooperatives exist among many small farmers in Tanzania because their operations are relatively small and scattered, and market outlets and resources needed for production supplies are often far away.

9.4.2 Education

Communication program is needed to make people establish a particular type of cooperative. The need for education applies especially to educators, legislators and the general public in order to decide on the type of cooperative to be established.

9.4.3 Pre-emption of the Field

If a non-cooperative business is not providing the desired services at a reasonable cost, the need for a cooperative may exist.

9.4.4 Institutional Factors

Institutional factors are important in establishing cooperatives. The cooperative legislations are necessary to call for cooperatives to be established in a country. In any given country the stability and continuity of a favorable governmental policy will do much to ensure successful cooperative business ventures.

Conclusion

The activities of cooperatives operating in the spheres of social and economic life show that it is possible to introduce cooperative methods of work in all sectors of the economy. Also, cooperatives are important not only for providing services to the members, but also to increase employment opportunities, thereby improving the standard of living for a large number of people.

A primary aspect of the importance of creating the conditions necessary for the well-coordinated and purposeful operations of cooperative organizations is the democratization of social life which will ensure members participate in making decisions to establish the type of cooperative to pursue their objectives.

References

Cliffe, L. Peter Lawrence,William Luttre, Shem Migot-Adhola and John S. Saul (eds.), 1975, *Rural Cooperation in Tanzania,* Dar es Salaam: Tanzania Publishing House.

Cooperative Union of Tanganyika (CUT), 1961, *By-Laws of Cooperative Union of Tanganyika Ltd.*, Dar es Salaam, Government Printer.

Forster, Peter G. and Sam Maghimbi, S. (eds.), 1992, *The Tanzania Peasantry: Economy in Crisis,* Aldershot: Ashgate Publishing Ltd.

Gordon. D., 1976, *Credits for small farmers in developing countries,* Colorado: Estview Press.

Hedlund, Hans, (ed.), 1988, *Cooperatives Revisited,* Uppsala: Scandinavian Institute of African Studies.

Hyden. G., 1980, 'Cooperatives and the Poor. Comparing European and the Third World Experience', *Rural Development Participation Review,* II: 1.

International Cooperative Alliance (ICA), 1973, Problems in the Development Consumer Cooperatives, Report on the proceedings of the Regional Seminar.

International Labour Organization (ILO), 1966, *Recommendations for Cooperatives,* No. 127.

Kimario, A.M., 1992, *Marketing Cooperatives in Tanzania. Problems and Prospects,* Dar es Salaam: Dar es Salaam University Press.

Kurt, R., 1969, *Agriculture cooperatives and markets in developing countries,* London: Fredric and Praeger Publisher.

Kruger, W. (ed.), 1967, *The Organization and Management of Cooperative Societies. Manual for Cooperative Officials,* Berlin: Union of German Consumer Cooperative Societies.

Lenin, V.I., 1977, 'Consumers and producers Cooperative Societies' in *Collected Works Vol. 32,* Moscow: Progress Publisher.

Luzzatts , Luigi, 1916, Selected speeches on *Cooperation and Economy,* Moscow: Progress Publishers.

Maghimbi, S., 2008, Consultancy Report on Cooperatives in Tanzania Mainland.

Marx, K., 1986, *Capital Vol. II,* Moscow: Progress Publishers.

Marx, K., 1986, *Capital, Vol. III,* Moscow: Progress Publishers.

Maslennikov, V., 1990, *The Cooperative Movement in Asia and Africa. Problems and Prospects,* Moscow: Progress Publishers.

Ngeze, P.B., 1975, *Ushirika Tanzania,* Dar es Salaam: Tanzania Publishing House.

Okoro, Okere, 1974, *The Economic Impacts of the Uganda Cooperatives,* Nairobi: East Africa Literature Bureau.

Otto, S., 1969, *Cooperation and integration,* New York: Asia Publishing House.

Ponte, Stephano, 2002, *Farmers and Markets in Tanzania,* Dar es Salaam: Mkuki na Nyota Publishers.

Robertson, A.F., 1984, *People and the State, An Anthropology of planned Development,* Cambridge: Cambridge University Press.

Roy, P., 1969, *Agriculture and consumer cooperative today and tomorrow,* Illinois: The Interstate Printers and Publisher.

Sharada, V., 1986 *The Theory of Cooperation,* Bombay: Himalaya Publishing House.

Strickland. C., 1933, *Co-operation for Africa,* London: Oxford University Press.

Tourben, B., 1980, *Marketing Cooperatives and Peasants,* Uppsala, Uppsala Press.

United Republic of Tanzania, 1975, The Villages and *Ujamaa Villages (Registration, Designation and Administration)* Act, 197, Dar es Salaam: Government Printer.

Widstrand C.C., 1970, *Rural Development in East Africa,* Uppsala: The Scandinavia Institute of African Studies.

Young, C., 1981, *Cooperatives and Development,* Madison: University of Wisconsin Press.

10

Procedures for Organizing A Cooperative Society

There are procedures which are usually followed in order to establish a cooperative society. To plan to start a cooperative involves conducting a sequence of events. This chapter analyzes the procedures for organizing a cooperative society. The challenges which may be encountered in procedures of forming a cooperative society are discussed.

10.1 Reasons for Organizing a Cooperative

There are four reasons to establish a cooperative society:

Firstly, a cooperative may be formed to improve material living conditions of the members (United Republic of Tanzania (1991) Cap. 7). Secondly, a cooperative may enable members to satisfy their needs by providing services in business, education, transport, communication, as well as to providing consultative services to members in order to improve their business. Thirdly, to promote cooperative education among members and non-members to motivate them in cooperative business (United Republic of Tanzania (1991) Cap. 7 (1). Fourth, to increase capital resources by encouraging thrift, wise use of credit and preventing usury.

Cooperatives may also expand existing market opportunities if they have business experts to search for new markets for products (Kistler, A. 1984). In order to establish a successful cooperative, there should be objectives of the new cooperative as well as consideration of the legal, economic, and financial aspects of the cooperative business (Cook, M. 1993).

10.2 Factors to Consider in Organizing a New Cooperative

The need to form a cooperative comes from different sources. People who have experiences of other cooperatives may suggest forming their own cooperative. The idea to form a cooperative may also originate with a cooperative specialist. Individuals in a community can also propose to form their cooperative in order to solve their social and economic problems. A suggestion to form a cooperative society may come from larger cooperatives especially regional associations wishing to extend channels. The idea of setting up a cooperative is discussed by few people in the area and if the suggestion is accepted, preliminary meetings should be convened for discussion by more people in the area.

Preliminary meetings should include by people who have an idea about cooperative organization. These people can convince others of the common interest to organize a cooperative. The meetings will determine the common problems that need to be solved. If there is support and approval of the idea, a survey committee of people who can do business research should be formed to conduct study of the social and economic conditions under which the cooperative will be formed (Schaars, M.A. 1970: 12-13). The survey committee should conduct an economic survey to collect facts which can have important bearing upon the success or failure of the proposed cooperative society:

10.2.1 *The Potential Volume of Trade*

The survey committee has to find out if the cooperative will have enough business to meet its operating expenses and at the same time leave some margin of savings. The minimum volume of products depends on the area which will be served by the cooperative, the intensity of production within that area, and the amount of products which the potential members within that area can deliver.

10.2.2 *The Resources*

A cooperative needs resources such as land, buildings, and equipment to handle the estimated volume of products. The Committee has to ascertain the resources needed and decide whether the physical resources will be rented, purchased, or constructed. These matters have important bearing upon the amount of capital that will be required.

10.2.3 *Funds Needed to Begin Operations.*

If the volume of business and the cost of acquiring the necessary physical resources are known fairly accurately, then the amount of start-up funds needed can be estimated reasonably well. Sources of funding should be proposed by the survey committee.

10.2.4 *Operating Costs*

The committee should estimate operating costs to see whether any worthwhile savings can be realized. The survey committee may estimate what volume of products would be necessary to make the venture worthwhile for the members.

10.2.5 *Experience of Potential Members in Other Cooperatives*

Membership support for cooperative may be there if members have had some good experiences with cooperatives. If the member had little or no experience in cooperation, the beginning should be modest. (Schaars, M.A. 1970: 12-13).

10.2.6 *Assess the Potential Supplies*

The survey committee has to assess the potential supplies.

The market is analyzed for product supplies. The committee has to evaluate the potential sources of products and compare the type of products, the quality and prices of potential suppliers.

The survey committee may consult various sources such as colleges and universities, trade agencies, consulting firms and government officers to get more nformation on cooperatives (Roy, E.P. 1989). The kind and depth of the surveys vary depending upon the type of cooperative to be established. The survey investigates the potential costs and benefits of the cooperative to be established. The survey of the potential members is a very important part of establishing a cooperative since all activities in it depend on the effectiveness and commitment of the members. The survey committee has to estimate how many people will be potential members of the new cooperative.

The survey committee report should be submitted to a meeting of prospective members to be discussed. The meeting should be chaired by a person who has knowledge of cooperatives and has the respect of the founder members of the potential cooperative. The group should weigh both the advantages and the challenges of forming a cooperative. After all points presented have been discussed by the participants the chairperson should ask the meeting for a motion to organize the cooperative or postpone or terminate the idea of forming a cooperative. If the idea to organize the cooperative is accepted the meeting should appoint an organizing committee (Schaars, M.A. 1970: 14).

10.3 Challenges in Organizing a New Cooperative

In organizing a cooperative, the following challenges may be encountered.

10.3.1 Financial Challenge

The founder members of a cooperative may lack initial funds for implementing the procedures needed. Some of the financial stresses can be critical when funding the cooperative and if no sources are in place, the idea to form a cooperative may fail to proceed.

10.3.2 Competition Among Members

If members carry out similar types of business and share a similar customer base, the chances of members being competitors outside their cooperative increases. The need to share services in the cooperative decreases and hence the motivation for the cooperative idea is weakened.

10.3.3 Lack of Member Support

Members need to support their cooperative by paying initial costs, getting services from it, and attending meetings. If members see their cooperative as a competitor in future, they might not use its services. The cooperative will have difficulty in implementing and sustaining its business without member support.

10.4 The Functions of the Organizing Committee

The prospective cooperative members should vote to elect members of the organizing committee. The functions of the organizing committee consist of the following:

10.4.1 *Sign for Membership*

The organizing committee should call on prospective members to sign up for membership. In Tanzania, a primary cooperative society may be formed by ten or more persons except for a cooperative of specialized skills which can be formed by as little as four people. A person may not be a member of a primary cooperative society unless he/she has reached the apparent age of eighteen years and should be of sound mind. Other requirements for membership are the following:

a) He/she should be engaged in a trade or occupation which is relevant to the object of the cooperative society.

He/she should have a common need which the cooperative society seeks to satisfy.

b) He/she should be capable of paying membership fees and acquiring shares (United Republic of Tanzania (1991: Section 14).

10.4.2 *Prepare Business Plan*

The organizing committee prepares a plan for the operating procedures of the cooperative. The committee has to prepare operating costs including employees' salaries, utilities, taxes, depreciation, interest, and cost of office supplies. Again, a meeting has to be convened to discuss the plan by members and they would then vote to pass the plan. (Croots and Spatz, 1995: 10-11);

10.4.3 *Incorporation*

A cooperative has to be incorporated under the laws governing cooperatives. The State has a Cooperative Act under which a cooperative must incorporate. The organizing committee has to draft the articles of incorporation, which is a legal document filed with the government. Articles of incorporation specify the name of the cooperative, place of business, purpose and powers of the association, proposed duration of the association, and information about the capital structure (Rapp and Ely, 1996). The articles specify the minimum number of ten cooperative members and the number of board of directors and terms of office.

The articles must not conflict with any provision of the Cooperative Societies Act. Articles must state the objective of promoting the economic and social interest of cooperative members on a non-profit basis. A cooperative can be registered with or without liability;

10.4.4 The First Meeting of a Registered Cooperative

The members of the new registered cooperative must receive notice of their meeting showing the date, time and place of the first meeting. The usual business of this meeting is to adopt the by-laws.

By-laws specify operational practice and policy (Schaars, M.A. 1970: 94). The meeting adopts by-laws. The by-laws state how the cooperative will conduct business and must be consistent with the State statutes and the articles. By-laws include issues such as membership requirements, rights and responsibilities of members, voting system, how meetings will be called, how the board is structured to represent the membership, (given geographical distribution and size of the membership), the scope of business and functions of the cooperative. Directors may be elected to represent districts, based on membership density, to reflect commodities or services to be handled, or some other basis that provides equitable representation (Cook, 1993).

After adopting the articles of incorporation and by-laws, the procedure which follows is to obtain legal status for the cooperative. The Commissioner of Cooperatives has to be consulted for the procedures, to ensure they are in accordance, with the provisions of the Cooperative Societies Act. After obtaining legal registration of the new cooperative the next step is to hold the first general meeting of the new cooperative. The first meeting after registration of the cooperative also elects the board of directors. These are members of the committee of the cooperative society who will run the day-to-day business of the cooperative. The board of directors is the governing body of the cooperative. The directors/ committee members range from four to fourteen members. The main function of the board of directors/committee of the cooperative is to establish specific operating policies and supervise the management of the cooperative. The board implements policies voted by the members' general meeting. Act (Schaars, M.A. 1970: 14-15).

The board of directors hires the senior officers of the cooperative: the Manager, Secretary, and Treasurer. The manager is the Chief executive to manage the cooperative. The board of directors should decide on staff salaries, job specifications, and working regulations of the employees. The board of directors must also develop an educational and training program for board members, employees, and cooperative members.

The board of directors also makes decisions on credit and pricing, purchasing, marketing and service policies as well as decisions on construction, trucking and warehouse policies. The board of directors must find investment funds. This has to do with capital that will be used to start the operation of the cooperative. Different sources can be considered including member investment needed to carry out the business plan; and

10.4.5 Begin Business

The cooperative should to operate on the basis of principles of cooperatives. There are rules for the successful formation of a cooperative. They include effective use of committees, keeping members informed and involved, maintaining good board/manager relations, following sound business practices, conducting businesslike meetings, and forging links with other cooperatives (Rapp and Ely, 1996).

Conclusion

The procedures for establishing a cooperative include the following: Firstly, to hold exploratory or preliminary meeting(s) with people of similar interests and determine the need to form a cooperative. Secondly to select a survey committee of people who can do business research to conduct survey of potential members, make market analysis for the products, supplies, and services and present the survey report in a meeting of potential members. Thirdly, to create an organizing committee to solicit more people to join as members of the cooperative, prepare articles and by-laws, incorporate the cooperative elect the board of directors and get funds to invest and carry out the business plan. The board of directors hires the manager and other senior officers of the cooperative and acquires facilities and equipment to begin business operation. Management and other employees oversee the day-to-day activities for successful cooperative business.

Cooperatives can help people in marketing their products or services to consumers. Cooperative marketing facilitates bulk selling and buying of products, and uses employees who have greater commercial skills than the member-producers. Well-organized cooperatives can improve members' economic power in bargaining for better marketing conditions and prices. They are a source of solidarity and incentives for improving the small farmers' social image.

References

Abrahamsen, M. A., 1976, *Cooperative Business Enterprise,* New York: McGraw-Hill Book Company.

Cook, M., 1993, *Consumer Cooperatives: Steps in Organizing a New Pre-Order Food Cooperative,* Missouri: University of Missouri Extension.

Croots, A.C. and Spatz, J.K., 1995, Basics of organizing a shared services cooperative, US Department of Agriculture, Service Reports: 46.

Dimoso, A.S., 1983, Impact of policy changes on the cooperative movement in Tanzania, M.A. Dissertation presented to the University of Dar es Salaam.

Kistler A., 1984, Annals of the American Academy of Political and Social Science: Union Organizing: New Challenges and Prospects, *The Future of American Unionism,* Vol. 473, New York: Sage Publication.

Kruger, W. (ed.), 1967, The Organization and Management of Cooperative Societies, *Manual for Cooperative Officials,* Berlin: Union of German Consumer Cooperative Societies.

Mufflin, H., 2004, *Cooperative Life: Starting a Cooperative,* New York: Houghton-Mifflin Company.

Ngeze, P., 1984, *Uongozi na Uendeshaji wa Vyama vya Ushirika,* Dar es Salaam : Swala Publications.

Okereke O., 1974, *The Economic impact of the Ugandan Cooperatives,* Kampala: East Africa Literature Bureau.

Rapp G. and Ely G., 1996, *Cooperative Information: How to Start a Cooperative,* New York: Rural Business Cooperative Services Ltd.

Roy, Ewel Paul, 1969, *Cooperatives Today and Tomorrow,* Danville: The Interstate Printers and Publishers Inc.

Schaars, Marvin A., 1971, Cooperatives, *Principles and Practices,* Madison: University of Wisconsin Press.

United Republic of Tanzania, 1982, *Cooperative societies Act No.5,* Dar es Salaam: Government Printer,.

United Republic of Tanzania, 1991, *Cooperative Societies Act No. 15,* Dar es Salaam: Government Printer.

Young, Sherman Rose, 1991, *Cooperatives and Development,* Madison: University of Wisconsin Press.

11

Managing Rural Cooperative Societies

Management is the science of combining ideas, facilities, processes, materials and labour to produce materials and services by an organization (Roy, E.P 1969: 426). Cooperative management is more than being technically competent. Cooperative management is of dual character in the sense that the member patrons are also the cooperative owners. The actors, processes, and issues in running and managing rural cooperatives are discussed in this chapter.

Cooperative management is a process of decision making and controlling the activities of the cooperative for the purpose of achieving the goals and objectives of cooperative society. The management process in cooperatives involves the member owners, the board of directors, the management staff, and the employees.

11.1 Concept of Cooperative Management

Cooperative management fosters free circulation of information within the organization through establishing, supporting, and rewarding behaviors based on trust and mutual help. The best interest is that of cooperative actors in order to induce them into participating by mobilizing human skills, processes, as well as financial and technological resources so that the goals of the cooperative can be reached (International Labour Office 1968: 8).

Management of cooperatives is an activity done by members, the board of directors, managers and employees. This relationship involves:

a) Ownership and control of a cooperative by members;

b) Efficient management by management staff;

c) Competent direction by the board of directors of cooperative society; and

d) Employees implement activities planned (Schaars, M.A. 1970: 17).

Cooperative management is essentially collective management.

a) There is election of a board of directors of a cooperative according to the principle of democratic participation and control;

b) There is collective decision making process on all cooperative plans, tasks and measures to attain the goals and objectives of a cooperative society;

c) There is collective responsibility and accountability by the board of directors who hire managerial staff and give guidelines to management on operational policies, goals and objectives of the cooperative organization; and

d) Individual employees and members are responsible of implementing the decisions and plans made in the collective management process (Kruger, W. (ed.) 1967: 36).

11.2 Rules in Cooperative Management

a) No person can be a member of more than one rural cooperative society without prior consent of the Registrar for Cooperatives;

b) No cooperative member shall hold more than one fifth of the share capital issued and paid of the cooperative society;

c) Individual persons may not be members of a cooperative union whose members are primary cooperative societies;

d) The promotion of economic interests should be in accordance with cooperative principles and objectives; and

e) No registered cooperative shall fix any limit to the number of its members (United Republic of Tanzania, (2005) Section 61).

11.3 Cooperative Members

The control of the affairs of a registered society should be vested in the general meeting summoned in accordance with the by-laws of the society and the Cooperative Acts (The United Republic of Tanzania (2005) Section 61(1)). Members participate in general meetings and make decisions on policies, finances, rules, election and their cooperative business. Members pass, adopt and amend by-laws and articles of incorporation. They pass resolutions and motions. Members have the mandate to elect the board of directors and be elected as directors of the board of the cooperative.

Members delegate powers to the board of directors to make decisions on their behalf. Members retain their right to approve the policies, budgets, audit reports, and plans of the cooperative. Members are responsible for providing the necessary capital, patronizing the cooperative to the fullest possible extent, paying the cost of operations, assuming the business risk, and keeping themselves informed about the cooperative. In order to control the cooperative, members must be active in their general meetings. Members must elect reliable and capable people to represent them in the board of directors. Members retain the right to approve matters of high and broad policy and to review the actions of their board and management. The annual meeting is held to give members an opportunity to legislate new policies, to review the results of previously adopted policies and to make changes in the plan of operations.

The board of directors and managerial staff report to the members of the cooperative at an annual meeting. A clear financial statement should be part of this report. The members are given audited financial reports. At the annual meeting the board and the manager should present to members the budgets and plans for the coming financial year. The by-laws should provide for calling special meetings for members whenever it is deemed advisable by the board or committee, or by one third of the total number of members of the cooperative. Thus, cooperative members exercise their control only in legally held meetings. The voting power of members is equal through the one-member, one-vote principle (Schaars, M.A. 1970: 18).

11.3.1 Membership in Cooperatives

The board of directors of the cooperative should review the applications for membership and accept or reject them in view of membership qualifications, which are:

a) That person has attained the minimum age of eighteen years and is of sound mind;

b) That person is following a trade or occupation relevant to the society's objectives as defined in the by-laws;

c) That person has a common need which the society seeks to satisfy;

d) That person is capable of paying fees and acquiring shares; and (The United Republic of Tanzania (2005) Section 15(2))

Cooperative members should receive education on cooperative principles and practices. They should be informed that they are legal owners of their Cooperative Society and they should receive benefits from the cooperative business.

11.3.2 Powers of the Members of Cooperative

Members of cooperatives have powers in accordance with by-laws, articles of incorporation, and the Cooperative Societies Acts. Cooperative members have powers to do the following things in their general meetings:

a) Amend and adopt by-laws;

b) Elect and recall directors of their board of directors;

c) Vote for appropriation of money for various purposes, to decide on business practices and contractual arrangements;

d) Require directors and management staff to run the business legally and according to the by-laws, articles of incorporation, and Cooperative Societies Act;

e) Examine annual reports;

f) Vote to approve plans and budgets; and

g) Appoint committees to examine or audit books and business records.

11.3.3 Responsibilities of the Members of Cooperatives

Members of a cooperative society have the following responsibilities:

a) Members have to provide appropriate share of the necessary capital and require an accounting report every year;

b) Members are the owners of the cooperative and they are responsible for the control of the organization and its management. Therefore, members should make sound policies concerning their cooperatives. Members adopt and amend by-laws and articles of incorporation as well as pass resolutions and member motions in their meetings;

c) Members should patronize their cooperative. The member patrons must bear the risks, if any, of their cooperative business, and each member bears a share of the risk proportional to equity and patronage;

d) Members pay the operating costs in proportion to the business which they transacted through the cooperative; and

e) Members are obliged to maintain the cooperative by supporting it all the time, especially when it faces business difficulties such as price crises.

11.4 Board of Directors of the Cooperative

The board of directors is the governing body in the cooperative. The board members are elected by cooperative members to act as representatives because all members of the cooperative cannot run the cooperative. A good board/committee is the cornerstone of the success of the cooperative.

11.4.1 The Powers of the Board of Directors of a Cooperative

a) Approve applications for membership and prescribe how to keep membership records;

b) Prescribe the form and extent of financial reports to members.

c) Make changes in the by-laws;

d) Borrow money for the cooperative from other sources and to decide upon the investments in the business;

e) Employ or dismiss the general manager and senior staff and determine their responsibilities, duties and compensation;

f) Call special meetings of the cooperative;

g) Employ an auditor or accountant as needed;

h) Declare dividends on stock and patronage refunds on business volume; and

i) Select a bank for the cooperative society's account.

11.4.2 Responsibilities of the Board of Directors of a Cooperative

The board of directors has the following responsibilities:

a) Prepare business plans;
b) Formulate policies consistent with the objectives of the cooperative;
c) Select a competent manager and senior staff and state their powers, duties, and rights;
d) Implement policies voted by the members in the general meeting;
e) Raise capital, borrow funds, and supervise disbursement of funds and direct the manner of distributing patronage refunds;
f) Select banks and qualified auditors;
g) Keep records of all board meetings;
h) Establish policies for employees' salaries, retirement, and other fringe benefits;
i) Evaluate business performance and plan for future operations;
j) Strive for efficient and competitive operation; and
k) Direct the manager to prepare an operating budget and present it for board/committee scrutiny (Schars M.A. 1970: 19).

The board of directors of a cooperative should not interfere in the daily operation of the business but should determine with members the policies of operation and check to see how these policies are carried out. The board should know the financial situation of the cooperative and ensure that financial records are kept accurately. The board should keep members informed about the cooperative business and the organization itself should be permeated with the spirit of service and respect to members.

11.4.3 Election of the Board of Directors of a Cooperative Society

The candidates to be directors of a cooperative should have the appropriate qualifications which cooperative members should consider during the election of board of directors. Members should elect directors who have good business outlook and are active in the cooperative and who are willing to serve in the board of directors of the cooperative. Members should elect directors who are articulate in expressing their opinions and who are able to analyze issues and abide by majority decisions. The directors should be able to work with others and should have sound business judgment (Schaars, M.A. 1970: 20).

The minimum number of directors on the board of directors of a cooperative society is stated in the Cooperative Act. In Tanzania board of a registered society should consist of not less than five members and not more than nine members including the Chairman and Vice-chairman (United Republic of Tanzania 2005: Section 63(1). An extremely large board is cumbersome and expensive to maintain. A small board of competent directors is more vigorous and effective. Members nevertheless can set the size of the board above the required minimum (Roy, E.P. 1969: 429).

The board of directors is elected during a general meeting called for that purpose. Election of the board of directors may be done by nomination from the floor. This may seem to be a convenient method but may not necessarily be the best way to get a board representative of the members. Another method of electing board of directors is to use a nominating committee. This committee prepares a list of candidates, preferably at least two nominees for each open position in the board. The nominations are made with consideration to representing different areas where the members live and individual qualifications to secure a well-balanced and able board. The nomination committee can judge the merits of the existing board members for re-nomination. The nominating committee should consist of three to five members who are familiar with the qualifications of a director as stated in the Cooperative Societies Act, the articles of incorporation, and the by-laws of a cooperative. Former directors should make good members for the nominating committee. The management, staff and current members of the board seeking re-election should not serve in the nomination committee.

Voting by secret ballot is preferable to voting by acclamation. Voting by proxy is not allowed by the Cooperative Acts in Tanzania. Proxy voting is a written authorization empowering another person to vote for and act on behalf of a member. In Tanzania, the elected board of directors shall hold office for a period of up to nine years provided that, in the case of those members of the board elected at the first general meeting of the society, one third of such members shall be voted out at the general meeting after the expiration of a period of three years from the date of their election, and one half of the remaining members shall be voted out after expiration of a period of six years from the date of election, and the remaining third shall leave office at the end of a period of nine years (United Republic of Tanzania (2005) section 63 (2)). For the purpose of the provision to subsection (2), the general meeting shall vote in one third of the new board members at the end of a period of 3, 6 and 9 years (United Republic of Tanzania (2005) Section 63(3).

Roy, E.P. (1969) suggests that the board of directors should be active and hold regular meetings, preferably monthly. Board meeting attendance allowance is an incentive to directors. To improve efficiency, the board of directors of a cooperative society may have sub-committees to deal with particular functions such as finance, buildings and equipment, marketing, and other functions. (ILO 1968: 24-28).

11.5 Management Staff of the Cooperative

The board of directors hires a general manager for a cooperative society. The manager should be experienced at understanding and using the expert knowledge of the technicians on the staff. The manager must be able to choose qualified subordinates and motivate them to work as a team and still retain authority over them. The manager must be able to work with the board of directors of the cooperative without becoming either domineering or unduly subservient (ILO, 1968: 38).

11.5.1 Powers of the Manager of a Cooperative

a) Hire and fire employees in the subordinate positions according to the general policy established by the board of directors;

b) Make periodic reports to the board of directors and recommendations on the cooperative's operations;

c) Plan, organize, coordinate, and control all administrative and financial operations of the cooperative;

d) Train employees for greater efficiency;

e) Supervise, conduct, and direct all activities as delegated to the manager; and

f) Represent the cooperative to the public as the board may direct.

11.5.2 Responsibilities of the manager of a cooperative

a) Supervise the operations of the cooperative in accordance with the policies agreed by the board of directors of the cooperative;

b) Maintain a good bookkeeping and accounting system and provide for examination by competent auditors selected by the board of directors;

c) Present at the general annual meeting a statement of the financial condition of the cooperative;

d) Attend all meetings of the board of directors and make a business report and periodic financial statement available;

e) Prepare budgets on income and expenditure and present them to the board as it may require; and

f) Confer with the board of directors on the development of new policies and appraise the effectiveness of policies already adopted.

The job of the manager is to serve member patrons efficiently, courteously, competitively and to delegate tasks to other cooperative employees. A good cooperative manager should have intellectual ability, technical and administrative competence, and a creative and visionary ability to look ahead at the trends in the business. The manager needs both technical and executive skills. Technical skills help to solve problems related to physical and inanimate resources; executive skills help to solve problems of human resources related to members, employees and the public.

The board of directors of the cooperative leans upon the manager, for advice and counsel related to board actions. The manager and staff are frequently asked to furnish information upon which policy decisions are based. Managers are best acquainted with details of operations, and thus are often able to appraise the feasibility of proposals. From this, it is clear that there should be a close working relationship between the board of directors and the manager (Schaars, M.A. 1970: 21-22).

The manager must communicate the cooperatives goals to all personnel; develop and direct marketing activities; select, supervise and support employees and uphold the cooperative's policies. The manager builds and maintains a positive relationship with members, other cooperatives, and the business community. The success of the cooperative to a large extent depends on its management staff. If there is good management that reflects the cooperative principles, success will be enhanced whereas in the opposite case the cooperative will fail.

Cooperative management is often faced with some problems such as those related to political and government intervention. Historically, it was because of political and government intervention that cooperatives in Tanzania, which were performing well in the early 1960s, lost direction and started performing poorly in the 1970s and 1980s. Political intervention has tended to tamper with cooperative management as a whole and disturbed the whole process in terms of how to run and manage cooperatives.

The position of the manager of a cooperative society should be filled by the most capable applicant. The general manager of a cooperative should be the most highly paid person in the cooperative. So in the process of selecting a person to fill this post, the board of directors should advertise the vacancy and specify the required qualifications, nature of the job, and remuneration package. The vacancy advertisement should appear in the print media as well as in electronic media and application forms should be made available to all prospective candidates. A special board meeting should be called to screen the applications and supporting documents, interview the applicants and select a manager. Finally, salaries paid by cooperatives should be competitive enough to attract and retain management that can attain the goals and objectives of the cooperative. Compensation methods could include salaries, commission on sales, and other fringe benefits including terminal benefits, and allowances as the board of directors may direct.

11.6 Employees of a Cooperative

The success of a cooperative society is often due to capable and honest employees. Sometimes principles of cooperatives are discussed as though adherence to them assures success. Such devotion to ideals generally overlooks the highly practical aspects of hiring good employees.

Employees are the key link between management, members, and the board of directors. Employees can make a cooperative successful if they are devoted. They should perform their duties according to regulations and procedures stipulated in the Cooperative Act and the cooperative's by-laws, those outlined by management, and those of the board of directors. Employees fill various positions in the cooperative such as those of cleaners, security guards, store keepers, drivers, cashiers and bookkeepers, and all employees are answerable to the general manager. Employees should work with full commitment for the realization of the goals and objectives of the cooperative. They should participate in the daily activities to make the cooperative a reliable business organization.

In the process of hiring employees, appropriate recruitment procedures should be followed. Candidates should submit applications for employment, and the applications, together with supporting documents, should be screened and applicants interviewed in order to hire those who are most qualified for the positions. Hired employees should work for a probation period of a year before they are confirmed in the tenure of employment. Employees should be informed about the cooperative and their work and they should be given the work rules and regulations and job descriptions. The management has to make clear from the beginning of employment what employees are supposed to do and provide on the job training. Management has to inspect employees' work regularly to ensure that it is done well and if there are weaknesses in performance, they should be overcome through proper guidance and training.

Cooperatives face various malpractice challenges such as corruption carried out by committee members and managers and fraud. These malpractices hinder a cooperative's goals and objectives. Lack of government support offered to cooperatives is another challenge. During the First Five Year Social and Economic Development Plan (1964-1969), the Tanzanian government implemented a policy that planned to promote and support the cooperative movement through staffing, supervision, and financial support. The situation changed with the introduction of free market and liberal policies in the 1980s, through which the government left cooperatives to run themselves. Government financial assistance to cooperatives ceased and cooperatives had to raise funds to pay for services and cover operational costs.

The challenge of stiff competition between cooperatives and private businesses with similar marketing businesses is also something cooperatives face. For instance, cooperatives compete with private companies in buying cash crops from farmers. There has been a tendency for farmers to be more willing to sell their crops such as coffee, cotton and other crops to private products buyers who pay farmers cash for the crops on delivery instead of selling to cooperatives, which make advance payments for the crop purchases pending making final payment as patronage refunds or second payment to members.

Conclusion

Success in running and managing cooperatives depends on the extent of integrity, honesty, and efficiency, coupled with technical and managerial ability of the board of directors, managers and employees. They must be willing to promote the work of the cooperative to see the fruits of cooperative business. Management should go beyond technical and administrative competence. The cooperative members, board of directors, managers, and employees should be involved in running the cooperative and be fully responsible in planning, organizing, motivating and controlling the cooperative society.

The board of directors and managers set goals and objectives for the day-to-day operations, design operating procedures and make financial projections. Managers are primarily responsible for the daily plans and projections. The cooperative employees must implement the tasks that accomplish the goals established by the board of directors. The managers prepare balance sheets and cash flow statements to be submitted to the board of directors and finally to the members' general meetings which receive, discuss, and make decisions based on such reports.

Managers are responsible for organizing operational processes, assets and personnel, A manager prepares organization charts to show employees work relationships. Communication flow on guidance and directives and feed-back on job performance are important in organizing work in cooperatives. Together with the organization charts the manager has to specify and describe the job allocations and show the expected levels of acceptable performance. Employees should implement business processes, programs and schedules to meet the cooperative's goals and objectives.

As chief executives in cooperative societies, managers should create good working conditions. Managers are responsible for staffing, training, and mobilizing personnel for job implementation. To improve work performance, there should be members' education and staff training. Training employees should uplift their status and prestige, and boost the employee's morale. Member education on cooperatives should focus on cooperative principles and practices so that members can be more informed about cooperative business. Employees' technical training is intended to improve their knowledge and skills in the work for which they are employed and eventually improve their efficiency and job output.

Managers exercise control to achieve good cooperative performance. Measuring and evaluating employees' performance should be conducted by managers in accordance with the goals and objective of the cooperatives. Together with overseeing and controlling performance, managers should oversee the physical assets and the financial condition of the cooperative so that they can achieve their goals and objectives (Abrahamsen, M.A. 1976: 268).

References

Abrahamsen, M.A., 1976, *Cooperative Business Enterprise,* New York: McGraw Hill.

Galen, R., 1995, *Field Operations, Cooperative Development,* New York: Department of Agriculture Rural Business and Cooperative Development.

Hyden, Goran, 1973, *Efficiency Versus distribution in East Africa Cooperatives,* Nairobi: East Africa Literature Bureau.

International Labour Office, 1968, Cooperative Management and Administration: Studies and Reports New Series 52, Geneva.

Kimario, Ally M., 1992, *Marketing Cooperatives in Tanzania. Problems and Prospects,* Dar es Salaam: University of Dar es Salaam Press.

Kruger, W. (ed.), 1967, *The Organization and Management of Cooperative Societies. Manual for Cooperative Officials,* Berlin: Union of German Consumer Cooperative Societies.

Lazo, Hector, 1937, *Retailer Cooperative,* New York: Harper and Brothers.

Lupogo, N., 2005, Members participation in managing and owning Cooperative unions in Tanzania: The case of the revived Karagwe District Cooperative Union.

Tungaraza, Felician, Mchomvu, A. and S. Maghimbi, 2002, 'Cooperative and Social Protection', *Journal of Social Development in Africa,* 17: 2.

Ngeze, P., 1975, *Ushirika Tanzania,* Dar es Salaam, Tanzania Publishing House.

Prokopenko, T., 1987, *Productivity Management,* Geneva: International Labour Office.

Roy, Ewell Paul, 1969, *Cooperative Today and Tomorrow,* Illinois: Interstate Printers and Publishers Inc.

Schaars, Marvin A., 1970, *Cooperative Principles and Practices,* Madison: University of Wisconsin Press.

The United Republic of Tanzania, 2005, *The Cooperative Societies Act. 2003 (Act. No. 20 of 2003). Revised Edition 2004,* Dar es Salaam, Government Printer.